RELIGIOUS ELEMENTS IN FAULKNER'S EARLY

NOVELS: A SELECTIVE CONCORDANCE

UNIVERSITY OF MIAMI PUBLICATIONS

IN

ENGLISH AND AMERICAN LITERATURE

NUMBER VIII   1965

RELIGIOUS ELEMENTS IN FAULKNER'S EARLY NOVELS:

A SELECTIVE CONCORDANCE

BY

GEORGE K. SMART

UNIVERSITY OF MIAMI PRESS

CORAL GABLES, FLORIDA 33124

PRINTED BY CENTER PRINTING CO., MIAMI, FLA., U.S.A.

For Virginia

ACKNOWLEDGMENTS

Permission to quote terms and their contexts from *Soldiers' Pay, Mosquitoes,* and *Sartoris* was generously granted by Random House. Faulkner's statements concerning the three novels and his early experiences with Biblical texts were taken with permission from interviews in *Writers at Work,* edited by Malcolm Cowley and published by the Viking Press.

Many helpful suggestions concerning the often difficult process of selection and arrangement were made by two of my colleagues in the English Department at the University of Miami—Professors John I. McCollum and Jack A. Reynolds. The project was encouraged in its early stages by Marjory Stoneman Douglas, Director of the University of Miami Press. Throughout the intervening months constant and sympathetic encouragement and assistance have been given me by Mrs. Jane Gaffin, former Acting Director of the Press, and Professor Reynolds, now Editor of the Press. Finally, the dedication of this volume to my wife, Virginia, can in no way compensate for her many and invaluable contributions to this study.

TABLE OF CONTENTS

INTRODUCTION

One of the most discussed questions in Faulkner criticism is the relation of his themes, characters, and his rhetoric to the Hebraic-Christian traditions. After the appearance in 1954 of *A Fable*, certainly one of the most ambitious efforts to use Christian materials in twentieth century literature, critical opinion has tended more and more to agree that the religious question is central in Faulkner's work.

There have, in general, been two widely different points of view in the discussion. One, developed at some length by Harry M. Campbell and Ruel E. Foster in the section of their study of Faulkner called "The Myth of Cosmic Pessimism," stresses the sardonic and ironic aspects of the religious or "cosmic" elements.[1] Other critics like C. Hugh Holman and Cleanth Brooks have found the spiritual tone to be essentially affirmative and related in a positive sense to what Professor Holman has termed a "nontheological interpretation" of Christian values.[2] In between these two polarities are all manner and forms of agreement and disagreement. As Brooks points out there are inevitable ambiguities and inconsistencies even within single episodes and single characters.[3] And Faulkner's own statements concerning the imaginative process make clear that the creative synthesis he seeks to achieve involves a multiplicity of elements and strands, and that in these the Christian tradition and Christian values are central.

> No one is without Christianity, if we agree on what we mean by the word. It is every individual's individual code of behavior by means of which he makes himself a better human being than his nature wants to be, if he followed his nature only. Whatever its symbol—cross or crescent or whatever—that symbol is man's reminder of his duty inside the human race. Its various allegories are the charts against which he measures himself and learns to know what he is. It cannot teach man to be good as the textbook teaches him mathematics. It shows him how to discover himself, evolve for himself a moral code and standard within his capacities and aspirations, by giving him a matchless example of suffering and sacrifice and the promise of hope. Writers have always drawn, and always will draw, upon the allegories of moral consciousness, for the reason that the allegories are matchless—the three men in *Moby Dick*, who represent the trinity of conscience: knowing nothing, knowing but not caring, knowing and caring.[4]

The feeling that Faulkner's use of religion is essentially bitter or sardonic is perhaps the more common. Irving Howe, for example, has said "Faulkner is a writer who has closely encountered Christianity but encountered it mainly in its decay."[5] But when one turns again to Faulkner's

1 Harry M. Campbell and Ruel E. Foster, *William Faulkner, A Critical Appraisal* (Norman, Oklahoma, 1951), pp. 114-140.
2 C. Hugh Holman, "The Unity of Faulkner's *Light in August*," *PMLA*, LXXIII (March, 1958), 166.
3 Cleanth Brooks, *William Faulkner: The Yoknapatawpha Country* (New Haven, 1963), p. 15.
4 Malcolm Cowley, editor, *Writers at Work: The Paris Review Interviews* (New York, 1958), p. 132. See also Joseph L. Fant III and Robert Ashley, editors, *Faulkner at West Point* (New York, 1964), pp. 95-97, where Faulkner says that everything a writer reads "from the telephone book up or down" may come into literary use. "Everything that happens to him he remembers, and it will be grist to his mill."
5 Irving Howe, *William Faulkner* (New York, 1951), p. 103.

own statements there is no commitment to a set pattern. Some years after the statements in the *Paris Review* interviews he emphasized the intimate associations with the Christian tradition in his early years. "I grew up with that, I assimilated that, took that in without even knowing it. It's just there. It has nothing to do with how much of it I might believe or disbelieve—it's just there."[6] This statement may perhaps add substance to the statement by Brooks that Faulkner accepts the Christian legend in substance but may at any time rebel against it,[7] and to the view of Professor John Hunt that Faulkner's viewpoint is both Christian and Stoic.[8]

If we take into account the pattern into which all these various views seem to fall—those explicitly stated by Faulkner and those of the major critics—it appears to represent a spectrum ranging from cosmic pessimism through irony and ambivalence to a qualified affirmation of Christian ethics. In studying the early work I have found these aspects of the spectrum far less varied. Indeed, in the sketches later published as *Mirrors of Chartres Street* the emphasis is almost entirely on a direct and literal use of religious terms and themes. In them one senses a conscious effort to develop the contrast between the failures and grotesques of the modern scene and the esthetics and spiritual traditions of Catholic New Orleans. The Fundamentalism of the various sects in the region of the Snopeses and the Benbows is almost completely left behind. And as Faulkner moved ahead to *Soldiers' Pay* and its Episcopal rectory there developed in the rhetoric and the characterizations a certain dialectic between the two traditions. *Mosquitoes*, although it is more completely identified with the New Orleans setting, similarly develops, especially in the rhetorical allusions and motifs a more somber conception of the failure of religious values to be more than empty and ironic phrases and tokens.

Then as he turned to the Oxford region of *Sartoris*, Faulkner demonstrated a far more engaged use of the contrast between religious ideals and worldly realities. The Christmas scene in the Negro cabin, near the end of the novel, is perhaps the first great passage in what was to become the Yoknapatawpha saga. Indeed Robert Cantwell has said that it is the scene "that sets the pattern for them all."[9]

It is beyond the scope of this study of the early novels to trace the subsequent development of this dualism, but it may be said in general that there is consistent extension of the primitive nontheological aspects of the Christian tradition so beautifully developed in the Christmas section of the third novel. We have it again in Lena Grove of *Light in August* and in Dilsey of *The Sound and the Fury*. This religious primitivism is often associated with the Puritan doctrine of the fall of man[10] and a recurring use of Puritanism in characterization and theme. As we move ahead to the later novels,

---

6 Frederick L. Gwynn and Joseph L. Blotner, editors, *Faulkner in the University* (Charlottesville, Virginia, 1959), p. 86.
7 Brooks, *op. cit.*, p. 41.
8 *Ibid.*, p. 373.
9 Quoted in Brooks, *op. cit.* p. 112. The statement was made in Cantwell's introduction to the Signet edition of *Sartoris*.
10 Brooks, *op. cit.*, p. 57, points out that Faulkner accepts the doctrine of original sin. He centers most of his discussion of Christianity in Faulkner's Yoknapatawpha series on this Puritan strain.

there is a growing sense of the symbolic and mythological substratum of religious themes. Indeed, the elaborate allegorical parable, *A Fable,* is perhaps more concerned with symbol and myth than with the Christ story which provides the structure and pattern of the novel.

All of these later developments show a widening and deepening of Faulkner's moral and philosophical view of man and his world. Yet a careful study of religious materials of the early novels seems to indicate that from the very beginning the Faulkner themes and the Faulkner tone grew to a remarkably significant extent out of the rhetoric, the symbols, and the motifs of Hebraic-Christian materials. Indeed, the allusions in each novel can be used to determine the literary qualities which Faulkner was exploring in the effort to establish what was to become a unique prose style, what may be termed the Faulkner mode or quality.[11]

There will apparently be no forseeable end to discussions of this aspect of Faulkner's work. The present study is designed to provide textual evidence which may contribute to a less speculative approach to the problem. It is a listing of terms and motifs which are related to Hebraic-Christian traditions, institutions, and values in the earliest novels. Included are references to Biblical accounts, the church and its many physical and spiritual aspects, motifs which may (and there are some which may be deemed doubtful) parallel the traditional religious themes, and the rhetorical devices which come from or reflect the language of religion. Purely mythological references are not included nor are references to the Oriental religions (which incidentally are sparse). Expletives or secondary profane expressions are listed in an appendix, some with only page and line numbers. The order of references is alphabetical, but within each entry so requiring it, the novels are referred to in order of publication. In addition, characters' names which have obvious (or perhaps only apparent) religious connotations, as for example the Semitic man of *Mosquitoes,* are included. In certain cases, there appear to be *double entendres* or ironic allusions, as in the case of Pete's halo-like hat in the same novel. Such references are also included. All references are to the first published editions of the novels.

It cannot be too strongly emphasized that this is a selective listing only. In general only the most explicit words, phrases, and motifs are included. They are identified by page and line, speaker and person addressed, by situation or subject when possible. Faulkner's own *obiter dicta* are so indicated. The length of the context passages varies from case to case as the rhetorical or thematic necessities seem to indicate.

That Faulkner's acquaintance with Biblical texts was of long standing may be seen by his statement in the *Paris Review* interview.

My Great-Grandfather Murray was a kind and gentle man, to us children anyway. That is, although he was a Scot, he was (to us) neither especially pious nor stern either: he was simply a man of in-

---

11 See especially Warren Beck, "William Faulkner's Style," and Florence Leaver, "Faulkner: the Word as Principle and Power," in Frederick J. Hoffman and Olga W. Vickery, *William Faulkner: Three Decades of Criticism* (Michigan State University Press, 1960), pp. 142-156; 199-211.

flexible principles. One of them was, everybody, children on up through all adults present, had to have a verse from the Bible ready and glib at tongue-tip when we gathered at the table for breakfast each morning; if you didn't have your scripture verse ready, you didn't have any breakfast; you would be excused long enough to leave the room and swot one up (there was a maiden aunt, a kind of sergeant-major for this duty, who retired with the culprit and gave him a brisk breezing which carried him over the jump next time).

It had to be an authentic, correct verse. While we were little, it could be the same one, once you had it down good, morning after morning, until you got a little older and bigger, when one morning (by this time time you would be pretty glib at it, galloping through without even listening to yourself since you were already five or ten minutes ahead, already among the ham and steak and fried chicken and grits and sweet potatoes and two or three kinds of hot bread) you would suddenly find his eyes on you—very blue, very kind and gentle, and even now not stern so much as inflexible; and next morning you had a new verse. In a way, that was when you discovered that your childhood was over; you had outgrown it and entered the world.[12]

And that this was a life long interest is made clear in his statement several months before his death in his discussion with faculty and students at the Academy at West Point: "I read in and out of the Old Testament every year."[13]

Concerning the three novels in general Faulkner has said this:

With *Soldiers' Pay* I found out writing was fun. But I found out afterward that not only each book had to have a design but the whole output or sum of an artist's work had to have a design. With *Soldiers' Pay* and *Mosquitoes* I wrote for the sake of writing because it was fun. Beginning with *Sartoris* I discovered that my own little postage stamp of native soil was worth writing about and that I would never live long enough to exhaust it, and that by sublimating the actual into the apocryphal I would have complete liberty to use whatever talent I might have to its absolute top. It opened up a gold mine of other people, so I created a cosmos of my own. I can move these people around like God, not only in space but in time too. The fact that I have moved my characters around in time successfully, at least in my own estimation, proves to me my own theory that time is a fluid condition which has no existence except in the momentary avatars of individual people. There is no such thing as *was*—only *is*. If *was* existed, there would be no grief or sorrow. I like to think of the world I created as being a kind of keystone in the universe; that small as that keystone is, if it were ever taken away the universe itself would collapse. My last book will be the Doomsday Book, the Golden Book, of Yoknapatawpha County. Then I shall break my pencil and I'll have to stop.[14]

---

12 Cowley, *op. cit.,* p. 136.
13 Fant and Ashley, op. cit., p. 66. See Faulkner's comment quoted p. iii *supra.*
14 Cowley, *op. cit.,* p. 141.

II

On the surface these three novels seem quite different one from the other. Yet they are remarkably similar in the frequency and character of religious terms and allusions. Even though *Soldiers' Pay* takes place for the most part in an Episcopal rectory, the other two are deeply infused with religious names and themes. For example, in *Mosquitoes* Faulkner chose to use throughout the name "Semitic man" for his philosophizing character Julius. Other characters include a David, a Mark, a Mrs. Wiseman, and a Josh. In *Sartoris* there are many references of churches, church officers, spirituals, and the culminating scene finds young Bayard in a manger-like stall at the Negro farmer's barn on Christmas Eve.

Two of the novels (*Soldiers' Pay* and *Sartoris*) are concerned with returning war veterans. It is perhaps more than coincidental that the great bulk of the profane expletives, the damns and hells, are spoken by embittered veterans or have direct reference to the war itself. *Mosquitoes*, while not as directly concerned with the war, is certainly a post-war novel, with similarities to the tone and type of characters of Eliot's *The Waste Land*.[15] The central section, which brings us the long and torturous ordeal of David and Patricia in the cypress swamp, is filled with overtones of martydom and crucifixion.

As to the character of the listings themselves, several comments may be made. First, they are often an important part of the fabric or texture of the rhetoric itself. The cedar and cypress trees, the church spire, the rectory garden, the Christmas scene in *Sartoris* all contribute significantly to the literary quality which is typically Faulknerian. Again and again, the phrases repeat almost literally, almost as if they were part of an incantation. Some lines (see especially under nave and peace) are so crowded with such effects that they generate unusual rhetorical intensity.

On the whole, the references are of a simple, commonplace homely sort. Literary allusions would be, of course, quite out of character for most of the dialogue, and although allusions, for example, to Dante and Beatrice and to *Paradise Lost* do occur, they are the exception. As Professor Holman has said, there is here an essentially nontheological vocabulary. It is in the symbolic motifs that broader meanings develop, not in the specifics of the language. It has often been pointed out that Faulkner's interest seems to lie in the Old Testament and in primitive rather than Pauline or spiritualized Christianity.[16] The references here listed seem to bear out this contention. Yet the aesthetic aspects of the religious vocabulary may be something in the nature of a rhetorical link between the two traditions.

Certainly one cannot conclude such a detailed analysis of the text of these first novels without seeing in them nearly all of the elements that contribute to the style and themes of the later novels.

---

15 Brooks, *op. cit.*, p. 105, comments on the Eliot influence demonstrated by the manuscript version of *Sartoris*
16 *Ibid.*, pp. 17, 40.

SOLDIERS' PAY AND MOSQUITOES

In his perceptive article on the religious aspects of *A Fable*, the German critic Heinrich Straumann concludes that Faulkner has in common with Fitzgerald "a negative evaluation of all attitudes tending to illusion" and that one of the sources of his dramatic effectiveness is "the suspension of his intellectual magnetic field between Manichaeism, Stoicism, and Christianity, and the meaningful references which are thoroughly worked out down to the smallest detail."[17] This statement interestingly enough might apply to the three early novels here analyzed. *Soldiers' Pay* is characterized by a sharp contrast between the forces of light and dark and the fatefully enforced asceticism of young Donald Mahon carries further the parallel to the doctrines of Mani. *Mosquitoes*, on the other hand, is pervaded with a spirit of Stoical and fatalistic acceptance of the ironies of the modern scene, following obviously the Stoical quality of the Eliot of the Waste Land period. Then in *Sartoris* we have the introduction of many simple and somewhat primitive Christian elements, notably in the Christmas scenes and the poignant flight and return of young Bayard near the end.

Turning to each of the novels now in more detail, we may note first that the opening section of *Soldiers' Pay* is characterized by a continuing sense of blackness and the forces of evil. The drunken soldiers returning on the train are in a crowded, frustrating kind of inferno in which the scarred face of Donald becomes more emphatic and cruel in its effect on the others. The colored porter, the dingy interior, the soot and dirt all carry out this effect. The language here is almost completely barren of poetic quality but is rather shot through with the profanity of the veterans. The expletives involving hell, damnation, and the like are not merely intensifiers but create the effect of a truly damned group of men.[18] The only hint of redemptive forces comes through the sympathy of the porter, of Gilligan, and gradually of Mrs. Powers, who is ultimately to break the circle of evil which seems to envelop the doomed protagonist.

When finally the scene changes to the rectory, the contrasting theme becomes more emphatic. The peace and beauty of the rectory, the aura of beneficence that surrounds Donald's father, the rector, and the natural beauty of the garden and the flowers bring the light and dark qualities into a more even balance.

One interesting aspect of the garden and the flowers is the recurrent use of the burning bush motif and of the grotesque and serpent-like Jones, with his yellowish eyes and almost amoral character. The allusions through this section often seem to suggest something of the Eden of the book of Genesis, in which of course Donald is a fatefully fallen Adam.[19] In some ways the garden seems to suggest the garden of Gethsemane, but again

---

17 Heinrich, Straumann, "An American Interpretation of Existence," *Anglia*, 1955, pp. 484-515, reprinted in Hoffma and Vickery, *op. cit.*, 349-372. The passage quoted is from the concluding paragraph.
18 See Appendix A for page and line references involved.
19 R. W. B. Lewis has traced this theme in American literature in his highly valuable *The American Adam* (Chicago, 1955).

in only the most general context. It is possible, of course, to see the rector as a divine being and Donald as a crucified son, just as critics have sometimes characterized the garden in Hawthorne's "Rappaccini's Daughter." In this analogy Mrs. Powers becomes a maternal figure, not so much the Madonna as a Mary Magdalene. Whether these quite speculative views can be accepted or not, and it may be added that such analogues continue to grow in significance in such subsequent novels as *Light in August*.[20] The allusions and motifs bear out the conception of this setting as religious and Biblical in rhetorical tone. The passages subsequently listed under burning bush motif perhaps best illustrate this tone.[21]

Other aspects of the allusions in the first novel are the quite specific references of the artifacts and the rectory, the candelabra, the vestments, and so on, which again are placed in sharp contrast to the satyr-like appearance of Jones and the flat and empty atmosphere of the settings outside the rectory. Similarly the characterization of Donald, the rector, and Mrs. Powers is in contrast to the treatment of Cecily and the other townspeople who tend to be two dimensional and flat. But the most striking aspect of the religious associations in the language itself is the development from the profane and sacriligious expletives of the opening section to the rich and symbolic religious allusions in the later sections of the novel.

Faulkner's second novel was in many ways a departure from the themes and symbols so effectively developed in *Soldiers' Pay*. Yet it has qualities quite unique in Faulkner's total work and in some ways more explicit uses of religious materials than is generally acknowledged. There are three settings or situations, each of which has a distinct rhetorical pattern. The major part of the novel takes place on the yacht Nausikaa. Here the tone is satirical and ironic. The names of two passengers are drawn from ironic Biblical analogues: Julius, who is nearly always referred to as the Semitic man and Mrs. Eva Wiseman. Other characters are named Peter, Mark, Joseph, and David. Sometimes Faulkner experiments with a certain effect of parody, as in the use of Pete's hat as a halo-like object. The discussions in which the Semitic man is involved tend to be stoical and skeptical in nature and indeed the whole novel has the quality of stoical acceptance that the Eliot of this period shared. Indeed, the Eliot influence is apparent, perhaps too apparent in the Prufrock-like Mr. Talliaferro and in the archetypal nature of the older passengers. The style of this section tends to be thin, dominated by dialogue and interrupted only once by a fantastic tall tale about Andrew Jackson and his half-man alligator swamp soldiers. Of the various devices employed, only the broad humor and exaggeration of this episode proved durable in the later novels. The parody fails and Faulkner seemed to have realized that straight parody and satire were not his forte.

Perhaps because of the shortcomings of the Nausikaa section, which was obviously an unsuccessful experiment, two other techniques develop.

<hr>

20 See Holman, *op. cit.*
21 See also "church bells" and "spire."

One is the long sequence in which the two young passengers, David and Patricia wander away while the yacht is aground and become lost in the cypress swamp. This section anticipates such later journey-quest narratives as the funeral trip in *As I Lay Dying* and Lena Grove's quest in *Light in August*. In this section the prose is enriched with references to the natural setting, which becomes symbolic in a style that verges on the stream of consciousness. As the two become exhausted there are crucifixion motifs and the cypress trees and the dim light tend to recreate the sense of a lost Adam and Eve driven from their Eden. The patriarchal swamp dweller who comes to their rescue carries this effect further and, indeed, the whole incident has a Biblical tone and aura.

Having tried now two quite different prose techniques, Faulkner obviously came to the realization that this second style—symbolic, allusive, rather religious in conception—was far the more congenial of the two. For in the final section, he employs it again, with more obvious use of the stream of consciousness, in the New Orleans night scene in which the Semitic man, the sculptor Gordan, and the novelist Fairchild wander about the streets in their own drunken search of a truth—or is it a grail?—which they cannot attain. They become now three priests, a kind of ironic trinity, and though they can attain only a stoical acceptance of life's limits and strains, they are Faulkner's vehicle for many religious and Biblical allusions. In this New Orleans section, the cathedral becomes part of the symbolic pattern and some of the passages echo the earlier sketches now known as *Mirrors of Chartres Street*.[22]

The second novel is, then, far more than a satire of the jazz age intellectuals. It reveals in many ways the process of Faulkner's stylistic development. The use of frontier tall-tale materials, the mythic and religious quality of the swamp scene, and the first extensive use of stream of consciousness passages were all to become integral parts of the Faulkner quality of the later periods. One final point should perhaps be made. In both of the other two novels use is made of the Negro spiritual and religious materials associated with the colored people. In *Mosquitoes* this is not the case, and the apparent difficulty Faulkner had in working with urban people in whatever way may have contributed to his decision to make use of the Oxford area in *Sartoris*.

SARTORIS

Despite the complete change in locale, the third novel retains many of the qualities of the earlier two. Young Bayard is in some ways reminiscent of Donald, and the townspeople react to his return in much the same way. The Sartoris home seems rather reminiscent of the rectory, an ironic place of refuge, and the frequent use of the cedar trees reminds us of the cypress trees which serve to create the somber atmosphere of the swamp scene in *Mosquitoes*.

---

22 See Appendix C where the language of these sketches is discussed.

But there is a conspicuous change in the use of religious terms and allusions. Perhaps the most notable is the extensive use of references to the religious practices and customs of the Negroes. In the earlier sections, these tend to be somewhat casual, although they serve to create a contrast between the simple, primitive acceptance of Christianity and these people and the searing doubt and guilt in young Bayard's mind. The death of his brother John, whose name has Biblical associations, in an Air Force plane referred to repeatedly as a Camel has plunged Bayard into a pattern of guilt and remorse which is juxtaposed with the naivete and light-hearted confident faith of the Negro servants.

This light-dark pattern is again reminiscent of the contrasting patterns in *Soldiers' Pay*, but it becomes more thoroughly developed as the novel progresses. For as young Bayard goes back into the country and stays with the family of boys of the MacCallum family, he returns in a symbolic and somewhat mythic sense to the innocence and dignity of a remote agricultural world. This section, done with a more completely engaged and emotive quality than anything in Faulkner's earlier work, has overtones of the ceremonies and events of the gospels. Indeed, the role of the father is almost god-like and the carefully developed mealtime scene becomes in a certain sense Bayard's Last Supper.

For a time this atmosphere of innocence and charity restores to Bayard some of the quality of *le chevalier sans peur et sans reproche* of the earlier Bayard of French legend. But the obsessive demon that drives him returns as he seeks his way back to Jefferson.

The primitive and mythological kingdom of the MacCallum's is left behind, but before he moves on toward the dark fate that is to come to him through the machine Bayard again experiences a mystical reenactment of primitive patterns. This comes about when he is forced to take refuge in a Negro family's stable during the Christmas observance. Again we find Faulkner moving toward the poetic and evocative language of the later novels. The Christmas customs and rituals are interwoven with the innocence and simplicity of the rural Negro people in a sustained passage of great rhetorical power. These passages are grouped in the concordance which follows under the word Christmas. An examination of them reveals the extent to which the combining of Christian and Negro customs and values adds a further dimension to the range of Faulkner's work.

It is, of course, this welding of regional religious traditions and a symbolic and mythological theme which led to Faulkner's later conception of such characters as Joe Christmas of *Light in August* and to the overall structure not only of that novel but of *As I Lay Dying* and *A Fable.*

Sartoris is, then, despite the echoes of earlier devices and themes, the beginning of what may be termed the major phase of his work. In this major phase, however, the use of religious elements remains constant, and as we have sought to point out in the discussion of *Mirrors of Chartres Street* in Appendix C, traces back through the early novels to sketches which were among his earliest efforts as a man of letters.

Selective Concordance of
Religious Terms Used In
Soldiers' Pay
Mosquitoes
Sartoris

ABRAHAM

Sartoris, 172:25[1]

With this foothold and like **Abraham** of old, he brought his blood and legal kin household by household, individual by individual, into town, and established them where they could gain money. (F re: Flem Snopes)

AEON

Soldiers' Pay 227:25

" 'For a moment, an **aeon,** I pause plunging above the narrow precipice of thy breast' and on and on and on." (Jones to Cecily)

AMEN

Sartoris, 274:28

". . . I hereby reinfests you wid yo' fawmer capacities of deacon in de said pupposed Secon' Baptis' Church. **Amen.**" (parson to Deacon Strother)

ANGEL

Mosquitoes, 139:4

The comb passed through her fair hair, with a faint sound as of silk, and her hair lent to Jenny's divine body a halo like an **angel's.** (F)

ANGELS

Sartoris, 9:16

. . . the history of the race had been raised from out the old miasmic swamps of spiritual sloth by two **angels** valiantly fallen and strayed,

---

[1] Page and line numbers, first edition. Faulkner's comments are those indicated by (F). For further explanation of entries see p. iii *supra*.

altering the course of human events and purging the souls of men. (F)

ARCHANGELS

Sartoris, 172:7

His voice became unintelligible, soaring into measured phrases which she did not recognize, but which from the pitch of his voice she knew to be Milton's **archangels** in their sonorous plunging ruin. (Narcissa re: Horace)

BAPTIST

Soldiers' Pay, 111:20

(Well, he's been closter to the Lord'n you'll ever git.)
This outer kindly curious fringe made way for Mr. Saunders.
(Closter'n that feller'll ever git, anyway. Guffaws.) This speaker was probably a **Baptist.** (townspeople and F)

Soldiers' Pay, 278:16

The **Baptist** minister, a young dervish in a white lawn tie, being most available, came and did his duty and went away. (F re: marriage of Donald Mahon and Mrs. Powers)

Soldiers' Pay, 295:10

(First, marched a uniformed self-constituted guard, led by a subaltern with three silver V's on his sleeve and a Boy Scout bugler furnished by the young **Baptist** minister, a fiery-eyed dervish . . .) (F re: Donald Mahon's funeral procession)

Soldiers' Pay, 298:7

(The sun had gone, had been recalled as quickly as a usurer's note and the doves fell silent or went away. The **Baptist** dervish's Boy Scout lipped his bugle, sounding taps.) (F re: funeral of Donald Mahon)

Sartoris, 272:19

"Brudder Mo'," he said, "will you read out de total emoluments owed to de pupposed Secon' **Baptis'** Church by de late Deacon Strother in his capacity ez treasurer of de church boa'd?" (the leader)

Sartoris, 274:24, 25

"Deacon Strother," he said, ez awdained minister of de late Fust **Baptis'** Church, en recalled minister of de pupposed Secon' **Baptis'** Church, en chairman of dis committee . . ." (the parson)

Sartoris, 274:27

". . . I hereby reinfests you wid yo' fawmer capacities of deacon in de said pupposed Secon' **Baptis'** Church." (the parson to Deacon Strother)

BEATITUDE

Mosquitoes, 339:24

"That's what it is. Genius." . . . "It is that Passion Week of the heart, that instant of timeless **beatitude** which some never know, which some, I suppose, gain at will, which others gain through an outside agency like alcohol . . ." (Gordon to Fairchild)

Mosquitoes, 341:2

He concentrated again, trying to exorcise the ravisher of his heart's **beatitude** by banging louder on the keyboard. (Fairchild's neighbor)

Sartoris, 25:14

He descended and tethered the horses, and his spirit mollified by the rebuke administered and laved with the **beatitude** of having gained his own way, Simon paused and examined the motor car with curiosity . . . (F)

BEATRICE

Mosquitoes, 339:8

Dante invented **Beatrice** creating himself a maid that life had not had time to create, and laid upon her frail and unbowed shoulders the whole burden of man's history of his impossible heart's desire . . . (F)

BELIEF

Mosquitoes, 184:6

"Dawson clings to his conviction for the old reason: it's good enough to live with and comfortable to die with—like a **belief** in immortality." (Mrs. Wiseman to Semitic man)

BELL (CHURCH)

Sartoris, 371:31

. . . all the peaceful scents of summer came up on the sunny breeze, the sounds—birds, somewhere a Sabbath **bell,** and Elnora's voice, chastened a little by her recent bereavement but still rich and mellow as she went about getting dinner. (F)

BELLS (CHURCH)

Soldiers' Pay, 61:1

The rector's great laugh boomed like **bells** in the sunlight, sent the sparrows like gusty leaves whirling. (F)

Sartoris, 372:25

When they reached town, from slender spires rising among trees, against the puffy clouds of summer, **bells** were ringing lazily. (F re: Miss Jenny and Isom)

BELLSTROKES

Mosquitoes, 14:24

The violet dusk held in soft suspension lights slow as **bellstrokes,** Jackson square was now a green and quiet lake in which abode lights round as jellyfish . . . (F)

BENEDICTION

Soldiers' Pay, 299:11

There was nothing harsh about this rain. It was gray and quiet as a **benediction.** The birds did not even cease to sing, the west was already thinning to a moist and imminent gold. (F)

BENIGNANCE

Sartoris, 60:6

Occasionally young Bayard or John would open the door and peer into the solemn obscurity in which the shrouded furniture loomed with a sort of ghostly **benignance** like albino mastodons. (F)

BIBLE

Mosquitoes, 27:2

Mrs. Maurier's voice faded and her face assumed an expression of mild concern. "Or is it the **Bible** of which I am thinking? Well, no matter: we dropped in to invite you for a yachting party . . ." (to Gordon)

Sartoris, 91:30

He . . . came upon a conglomeration of yellowed papers neatly bound in packets, and at last upon a huge, brass-bound **Bible.** He lifted this to the edge of the chest and opened it. The paper was brown and mellow with years, and it had a texture like that of slightly moist wood-ashes . . . (old Bayard)

Sartoris, 160:34

Three score and ten years to drag a stubborn body about the world and cozen its insistent demands. Three score and ten, the **Bible** said. Seventy years. And he was only twenty-six. (young Bayard)

Sartoris, 324:12

His spent blood, wearied with struggling, moved through his body in slow beats, like the rain, wearing his flesh away. It comes to all . . . **Bible** . . . some preacher, anyway. Maybe he knew. Sleep. It comes to all. (young Bayard)

BIBLICAL

Soldiers' Pay, 317:1

"Well, Joe, things are back to normal again. People come and go, but Emmy and I seem to be like the **biblical** rocks." (rector to Joe Gilligan)

4

BIBLICAL PLAGUE

Mosquitoes, 8:12

They came cityward lustful as country boys, as passionately integral as a football squad; pervading and monstrous but without majesty: a **biblical plague** seen through the wrong end of a binocular: the majesty of Fate become contemptuous through ubiquity and sheer repetition. (F)

BISHOP

Soldiers' Pay, 62:4

"So I left the bush uncovered . . . and repaired to the conference. The weather continued perfect until the last day, then the weather reports predicted a change. The **bishop** was to be present . . . (rector to Jones)

BLESS[1]

Soldiers' Pay, 170:22

"**Bless** de Lawd, done sont you back ter yo' mammy. Yes, Jesus! Ev'y day I prayed, and de Lawd heard me." (Callie to Donald Mahon)

Soldiers' Pay, 317:8

"God **bless** you, Joe. Was it on my account you decided to stay?" (rector to Joe Gilligan)

BLESSIN'

Sartoris, 113:8

"Hit's de Lawd's **blessin'** you and her ain't bofe gone in it, like you is whenever Mist' Bayard'll let you." (Elnora to Isom re: young Bayard's car)

BROTHER

Mosquitoes, 337:25

The begger yet sleeps, shaping his stolen crust, and one of the priests says, Do you require aught of man, **Brother**? (F)

Mosquitoes, 338:3

The beggar makes no reply . . . Beneath his high white brow he is not asleep, for his eyes stare quietly past the three priests without remarking them. The third priest leans down, raising his voice. **Brother** (F)

BURNING BUSH MOTIF

Soldiers' Pay, 61:16

Upon a lattice wall wisteria would soon burn in slow inverted lilac

---

[1] See also Appendix A, p. 129.

5

flame, and following it they came lastly upon a single rose **bush.** (F re: rector and Jones)

Soldiers' Pay, 61:17, 19
The **branches** were huge and knotted with age, heavy and dark as a bronze pedestal, crowned with pale impermanent gold. The divine's hands lingered upon **it** with soft passion. (F re: rector and the rose bush)

Soldiers' Pay, 61:20, 21, 23
"Now, **this,**" he said, "is my son and my daughter, the wife of my bosom and the bread of my belly: **it** is my right hand and my left hand. Many is the night I have stood beside **it** . . . burning newspapers to keep the frost out." (rector to Jones re: the rose bush)

Soldiers' Pay, 61:30
"The tips were already swelling. Ah, my boy, no young man ever waited the coming of his mistress with more impatience than do I the first bloom on this **bush.**" (rector to Jones)

Soldiers' Pay, 62:1
"So I left the **bush** uncovered against my better judgment and repaired to the conference." (rector to Jones)

Soldiers' Pay, 62:18
"This rose has almost made history. You have had the **bush** for some time, have you not? One does become attached to things one has long known." (Jones to rector)

Soldiers' Pay, 62:21
"In this **bush** is imprisoned a part of my youth, as wine is imprisoned in a wine jar. But with this difference: my wine jar always renews itself." (rector to Jones)

Soldiers' Pay, 63:10
"Man cannot remain in one position long enough to really think. But about the rose **bush** . . . " (rector to Jones)

CANDELABRA

Soldiers' Pay, 107:20
Across the garden, beyond a street and another wall you could see the top of a pear tree like a branching **candelabra** closely bloomed, white, white . . . (F)

CANDLESTICKS

Soldiers' Pay, 281:22, 23
Fruit blossoms were gone, pear was forgotten: what were once tall **candlesticks,** silvery with white bloom, were now tall jade **candlesticks** of leaves beneath the blue cathedral of sky . . . (F)

CATHEDRAL

Soldiers' Pay, 281:23

... tall jade candlesticks of leaves beneath the blue **cathedral** of sky across which, in hushed processional, went clouds like choirboys slow and surpliced. (F)

Mosquitoes, 14:5

... three spires of the **cathedral** graduated by perspective, pure and slumbrous beneath the decadent languor of August and evening. (Talliaferro viewing the twilight)

Mosquitoes, 14:28

Pontalba and **cathedral** were cut from black paper and pasted flat on a green sky; above them taller palms were fixed in black and soundless explosions. (F)

Mosquitoes, 48:33

There was a moon, low in the sky and worn, thumbed partly away like an old coin ... Above banana and palm the **cathedral** spires soared without perspective on the hot sky. (F)

Mosquitoes, 180:14

The road went on shimmering before them, endless beneath bearded watching trees, crossing the implacable swamp with a puerile bravado like a thin voice cursing in a **cathedral**. (F re: David and Patricia)

Mosquitoes, 305:1

Fairchild sat ... enjoying the cool darkness and the shadowed tree-filled spaciousness of the **cathedral** close beneath his balcony. (F)

Mosquitoes, 325:30

"They were married in the **Cathedral**." (Semitic man to Fairchild re: Mrs. Maurier and her husband)

CATHOLIC

Soldiers' Pay, 97:4

He was a **Catholic**, which was almost as sinful as being a republican ... (F re: Mr. Saunders)

Soldiers' Pay, 231:4

Jones grew up in a **Catholic** orphanage, but like Henry James, he attained verisimilitude by means of tediousness. (F)

Mosquitoes, 42:18

"For some reason one can be a **Catholic** or a Jew and be religious at home." (Semitic man to Fairchild)

7

Mosquitoes, 325:31

"She wasn't a **Catholic**—Ireland had yet to migrate in any sizable quantities when her people established themselves in New England." (Semitic man to Fairchild re: Mrs. Maurier)

Sartoris, 270:7

. . . the deputation came solemnly around the corner of the house from the rear. It consisted of six negroes in a **catholic** variety of Sunday raiment . . . (F)

CEDAR TREES

Soldiers' Pay, 160:2

The sun was yet in the tops of trees and here were **cedars** unsunned and solemn, a green quiet nave. (F)

Soldiers' Pay, 160:11

Her head was lowered and she dug in the earth with a stick. Her unconscious profile was in relief against a dark **cedar** . . . (Mrs. Powers)

Soldiers' Pay, 297:12

Away, following where fingers of sunlight pointed among **cedars,** doves were cool, throatily unemphatic among the dead. (F)

Sartoris, 153:29

The moon stood overhead; along the drive the **cedars** in a rigid curve were pointed against the pale, faintly spangled sky. (F)

Sartoris, 155:32

This third caller entered by a lane and mounted on to the wall and thence to the garage roof, where he now lay in the shadow of a **cedar,** sheltered so from the moon. (F)

Sartoris, 157:12

. . . all six of them drank fraternally from the jug, turn and turn about. At last they reached the Benbow's and played once beneath the **cedars.** (F re: callers who serenaded Narcissa)

Sartoris, 169:14, 14

From the gate the cinder-packed drive rose in a grave curve between **cedars.** The **cedars** had been set out by an English architect of the '40's, who had built the house . . . beneath and among them, even on the brightest days, lay a resinous exhilarating gloom. (F re: the Benbow home)

Sartoris, 169:26

The drive ascended to the house and curved before it and descended again into the street in an unbroken arc of **cedars.** (F re: the Benbow home)

Sartoris, 170:21

At the top of the drive . . . sat the doll's house in which Horace and Narcissa lived, surrounded always by that cool, faintly astringent odor of **cedar** trees. (F re: the Benbow home)

Sartoris, 175:28

Fireflies had not yet come, and the **cedars** flowed unbroken on either hand down to the street, like a curving ebony wave with rigid unbreaking crests pointed on the sky. (F)

Sartoris, 176:6

. . . Horace stood on the veranda with his cold pipe, surrounded by that cool astringency of **cedars** like another presence. (F re: the Benbow home)

Sartoris, 180:1

Then Horace was in school at Sewanee and later at Oxford, from which he returned just in time to see Will Benbow join his wife among pointed **cedars** and carven doves and other serene marble shapes . . . (F re: death of Will Benbow)

Sartoris, 352:1

Already the thick cables along the veranda eaves would be budding into small lilac match-points, and with no effort at all he could see the lawn below the **cedars,** splashed with random narcissi among random jonquils, and gladioli waiting in turn to bloom. (F re: Horace)

Sartoris, 373:22

Now and then they were surmounted by symbolical urns and doves and surrounded by clipped, tended sward green against the blanched marble and the blue dappled sky and the black **cedars** from amid which doves crooned, endlessly reiterant. (F re: Miss Jenny and Isom in the cemetery)

Sartoris, 374:29

The **cedars** had almost overgrown his son John's and John's wife's graves. Sunlight reached them only in splashes, dappling the weathered stone with fitful stipplings . . . (F re: old Bayard)

Sartoris, 375:21

The pedestal and effigy were mottled with seasons of rain and sun and with drippings from the **cedar** branches . . . (F re: the cemetery)

Sartoris, 376:6

The wind drew among the **cedars** in long sighs, and steadily as pulses the sad hopeless reiteration of the doves came along the sunny air. (F)

CELIBATE

Mosquitoes, 335:3

Three gray, softfooted priests had passed on, but in an interval hushed by windowless old walls there lingers yet a thin **celibate** despair. (F)

Mosquitoes, 340:14

The priests cross themselves while the nuns of silence blend anew their breath, and pass on: soon the high windowless walls have hushed away their thin **celibate** despair. (F)

CEREMONIAL (CHRISTENING)

Sartoris, 371:26

Narcissa and the nurse, in an even more gaudy turban, had brought the baby, bathed and garnished and scented in his **ceremonial** robes, in to her, and later she heard them drive away in the carriage . . . (F re: young Bayard's son and Miss Jenny)

CEREMONY (FUNERAL)

Soldiers' Pay, 296:17

But it seemed as if she could hear . . . the hushed scraping of timid footsteps, the muted thumping of wood against wood . . . an unbearable unchasity of stale flowers—as though flowers themselves getting a rumor of death became corrupt—all the excruciating **ceremony** for disposing of human carrion. (F re: Emmy)

CHAFF

Sartoris, 139:14

Above the stream gnats whirled and spun in a leveling ray of sunlight, like erratic golden **chaff.** (F)

CHANT

Sartoris, 7:19

. . . from somewhere beyond the bar of sunlight a voice rose and fell in a steady preoccupied minor, like a **chant.** (F re: a Negro)

Sartoris, 132:17

The negro glanced over his shoulder and crouched against the animal, and his crooning **chant** rose to a swifter beat. (F re: a Negro)

CHANTING

Sartoris, 7:23

The **chanting** ceased, and as he turned toward the stairs a tall mulatto woman appeared in the slanting sunlight at the back door . . . (F re: old Bayard and Elnora)

CHAOS

Mosquitoes, 47:5, 6

. . . form shapes cunningly sweated cunning to simplicity shapes out of **chaos** more satisfactory than bread to the belly form by a madmans dream gat on the body of **chaos** . . . (Gordon)

Sartoris, 48:5
. . . something of that magical **chaos** in which they had lived for two months, tragic and transient as a blooming of honeysuckle and sharp as the odor of mint. (F re: young Bayard and his first wife)

Sartoris, 136:4
. . . it seemed, for all its aloofness, to be a part of the whirling ensuing **chaos**; a part of it, yet bringing into the red vortex a sort of constant coolness like that of a faint, shady breeze. (young Bayard re: a face)

Sartoris, 307:1
The din of them swelled to a shrill pandemonium and the pack boiled into the road in a **chaos** of spotted hides and flapping tongues and ears. (young Bayard and dogs)

Sartoris, 323:34
. . . surrounded by coiling images and shapes of stubborn despair and the ceaseless striving for . . . not vindication so much as comprehension; a hand, no matter whose, to touch him out of his black **chaos.** (young Bayard)

CHAOTIC

Soldiers' Pay, 45:8
In the next room Cadet Lowe waked from a **chaotic** dream, opening his eyes and staring with detachment, impersonal as God, at lights burning about him. (F)

Soldiers' Pay, 223:7
"It would be the devil of a **chaotic** world if you never could count on whether or not people mean what they say." (Jones to Cecily)

Mosquitoes, 127:25
But he still felt eyes upon him and he stood acutely, trying to think of something to do, some casual gesture to perform. A cigarette his **chaotic** brain supplied at last. (Talliaferro)

Mosquitoes, 288:20
Again Mrs. Maurier's voice failed her, and her amazement became a **chaotic** thing that filled her round face interestingly. (F)

CHAPLAIN

Soldiers' Pay, 189:14
A **chaplain** appears who, to indicate that the soldiers love him because he is one of them, achieves innuendoes about home and mother . . . (F)

CHARTES

Mosquitoes, 320:16
"A perversion, I grant you, but a perversion that builds **Chartes** and invents Lear is a pretty good thing." (Fairchild to Semitic man re: art and creativity)

CHASTE

Sartoris, 94:26
. . . a soul hampered now by material strictures, but destined and determined some day to function amid Persian rugs . . . and a single irreproachable print on the **chaste** walls. (F)

Sartoris, 171:11
. . . the vase he had blown on shipboard—a small **chaste** shape in clear glass, not four inches tall, fragile as a silver lily and incomplete. (Horace)

CHASTELY

Sartoris, 182:14
. . . he had set up his furnace . . . and produced one almost perfect vase of clear amber, larger, more richly and **chastely** serene . . . (Horace)

CHASTENED

Sartoris, 371:32
. . . somewhere a Sabbath bell, and Elnora's voice, **chastened** a little by her recent bereavement but still rich and mellow as she went about getting dinner. (F)

CHERUBIC

Mosquitoes, 34:8
The **cherubic** waiter spun a chair from an adjoining table . . . (F)

Mosquitoes, 37:33
The **cherubic** waiter bent over them. (F)

CHERUBIM

Mosquitoes, 193:14
"Finish your drink. O immaculate **cherubim**," . . . (Semitic man to Fairchild)

Sartoris, 43:16
. . . John Sartoris slept among martial **cherubim** and the useless vainglory of whatever God he did not scorn to recognize. (F)

CHIMED

Mosquitoes, 13:22, 23
They were gone, hushing their **chimed** footsteps up the dark curve of the stair: their **chimed** tread was like a physical embrace. (Talliaferro re: a couple)

CHOIRBOYS

Soldiers' Pay, 281:24
. . . beneath the blue cathedral of sky across which, in hushed processional, went clouds like **choirboys** slow and surpliced. (F)

CHORAL

Sartoris, 371:10
. . . and the three of them would sit for rapt, murmurous hours in a sort of **choral** debauch of abnegation while the object of it slept . . . (F re: Narcissa, nurse, Miss Jenny and baby)

CHORD (RELIGIOUS MUSIC)

Soldiers' Pay, 318:26
. . . across a level moon-lit space, broken by a clump of saplings, came a pure quivering **chord** of music wordless and far away. (F re: Negroes)

CHORDS (RELIGIOUS MUSIC)

Sartoris, 148:6
. . . they stood with their heads together, murmuring among themselves and touching plaintive muted **chords** from the strings. (F re: Negroes)

Sartoris, 148:13
. . . they drifted in rich, plaintive **chords** upon the silver air, fading, dying in minor reiterations along the treacherous vistas of the moon. (F re: Negro tunes)

Sartoris, 280:25
Sometimes they sang—quavering, wordless **chords** in which plaintive minors blent with mellow bass in immemorial and sad suspense . . . (F re: Negroes)

CHRIST

Mosquitoes, 42:6
"But to go back to religion"—"the spirit protestant eternal," . . . "do you mean any particular religion, or just the general teaching of **Christ?**" (blond young man to Fairchild et al)

Mosquitoes, 42:7

"What has **Christ** to do with it?" (Fairchild to blond young man)

Mosquitoes, 48:1

stars in my hair in my hair and beard i am crowned with stars **christ** by his own hand autogethsemane carved darkly out of pure space . . . (Gordon)

CHRIST MOTIF

Mosquitoes, 137:20

The moon spread her silver hand on it; a broadening path of silver, and in the path the water came alive ceaselessly, no longer rigid . . . "The only **man** who could walk on water is dead." (Patricia to Jenny)

CHRISTENING

Sartoris, 371:22

She set the date before she went to bed and held to it stubbornly, refusing even to rise and attend the **christening**. (Miss Jenny and young Bayard's baby)

CHRISTIAN

Mosquitoes, 40:1

"No," the Semitic man agreed. "But, like any **Christian**, he would have liked the opportunity to refuse." (to Fairchild et al)

CHRISTIAN (YOUNG MEN'S CHRISTIAN ASSOCIATION)

Soldiers' Pay, 295:11

(First, marched a uniformed, self-constituted guard, led by a subaltern with three silver V's on his sleeve and a Boy Scout bugler furnished by the young Baptist minister, a fiery-eyed dervish, who had served in the **Y.M.C.A.**) (F re: funeral procession of Donald Mahon)

Sartoris, 31:18

"Horace must have got rich, like the soldiers say all the **Y.M.C.A.** did. Well, if it has taught a man like Horace to make money, the war was a pretty good thing, after all." (Miss Jenny to Narcissa)

Sartoris, 173:19

Later, to everyone's surprise, particularly that of Horace Benbow's friends, he departed with Horace to a position in the **Y.M.C.A.** (F re: Snopes)

CHRISTIANITY

Soldiers' Pay, 231:15

"Since then I have been a firm believer in **Christianity**." (Jones to Mrs. Saunders)

14

CHRISTIANIZED

Mosquitoes, 40:30
The Semitic man said: "My people produced Jesus, your people **Christianized** him." (to Talliaferro et al)

CHRISTMAS

Mosquitoes, 118:4
"So I had to give up one of my lecture courses, though the instructor . . . let me try to make it up during the **Christmas** vacation." (Fairchild to Josh)

Sartoris, 10:25
Aunt Jenny told the story first shortly after she came to them. It was **Christmas** time and they sat before a hickory fire in the rebuilt library . . . (the Sartoris family)

Sartoris, 11:7
"**Chris'mus!**" Joby exclaimed, with the grave and simple pleasure of his race . . .

Sartoris, 98:22
Everyone in the country knew him and sent him hams and wild game at **Christmas** . . . (Dr. Peabody)

Sartoris, 232:24
"Dat 'uz erbout las' **Chris'mus** time, en now dey wants de money back." (Simon to old Bayard)

Sartoris, 290:29
"You think, just because you've eaten off of us Thanksgiving and **Christmas** for sixty years, that you can come into my own house and laugh at me, don't you?" (Miss Jenny to Loosh Peabody)

Sartoris, 291:29
This was the pint flask of whisky which he included in old man Falls' Thanksgiving and **Christmas** basket . . . (F re: old Bayard)

Sartoris, 312:33
"Well, hit don't matter. You'll be goin' in next week, for **Christmas**," the old man said. (Mr. MacCallum to Rafe)

Sartoris, 333:10
Christmas was two days away, and they sat again about the fire after supper . . . (the MacCallum family)

Sartoris, 333:17
. . . he believed that in all their minds it was taken for granted that he would return home the following day for **Christmas** . . . (young Bayard at the MacCallum home)

Sartoris, 335:18

. . . they sat about the hearth with their bedtime toddies, talking of **Christmas.** (the MacCallum family)

Sartoris, 335:23

"With a pen full of 'possoms, and a river bottom full of squir'l and ducks, and a smokehouse full of hawg meat, you damn boys have got to go clean to town and buy a turkey fer **Christmas** dinner." (Mr. MacCallum to his sons)

Sartoris, 335:25, 25

"**Christmas** ain't **Christmas** lessen a feller has a little somethin' different from ever' day," Jackson pointed out mildly. (to Mr. MacCallum)

Sartoris, 335:30, 31

"I've seen a sight mo' **Christmases** than you have, boy, and ef hit's got to be sto'bought, hit ain't **Christmas.**" (Mr. MacCallum to Jackson)

Sartoris, 335:33

"How about town folks?" Rafe asked. "You ain't allowin' them no **Christmas** a-tall." (to Mr. MacCallum)

Sartoris, 336:12

"Why, you fellers don't know nothin' about **Christmas.** All you knows is sto' winders full of cocoanuts and Yankee popguns and sich." (Mr. MacCallum to his sons)

Sartoris, 343:25

Before he slept he uncovered his arm and looked at the luminous dial on his wrist. One o'clock. It was already **Christmas.** (young Bayard in the stall)

Sartoris, 344:17

"**Chris'mus** gif', white folks," he said, eying the jug. (Negro to young Bayard)

Sartoris, 345:7

"Had your **Christmas** dram yet, aunty?" (young Bayard to Negro)

Sartoris, 345:14

The three children squatted against the wall, watching him steadily, without movement and without sound. "**Christmas** come yet, chillen?" (young Bayard to Negro children)

Sartoris, 346:3

The children now played quietly with their **Christmas,** but from time to time he found them watching him steadily and covertly. (young Bayard and Negro children)

Sartoris, 346:18

"You's in a powerful rush fer **Chris'mas,** white folks." (Negro to young Bayard)

Sartoris, 346:25

"I ain't had no **Chris'mus** yit, white folks." (Negro to young Bayard)

Sartoris, 346:26

"Feller workin' ev'y day of de year wants a little **Chris'mus.**" (Negro to young Bayard)

Sartoris, 347:16

The negroes drank with him . . . humankind forgetting its lust and cowardice and greed for the day. "**Chris'mus,**" the woman murmured shyly. "Thanky, suh." (Negroes and young Bayard)

Sartoris, 348:6

"Heyo, **Chris'mus!**" Beyond the yellow sedge and brown ridges the ultimate hills stood bluely against the plumbless sky. "Heyo." (Negro to young Bayard)

Sartoris, 349:5, 6

It looked the same way at home . . . drinking a little and shooting fireworks and giving nickels and dimes and quarters to negro lads who shouted "**Chris'mus** gif'! **Chris'mus** gif'!" (young Bayard)

Sartoris, 349:11

. . . Simon entering his and Johnny's room on tense and clumsy tiptoe and holding his breath above the bed . . . whereupon they both roared "**Christmas** gift!" (young Bayard)

Sartoris, 350:17

As he turned here a voice spoke diffidently from the shadow beside the door. "**Chris'mus** gif', boss." (Negro to young Bayard)

CHRISTMAS EVE

Sartoris, 60:14

. . . the room would be opened only on **Christmas Eve,** when the tree was set up and a fire lighted, and a bowl of eggnog on the table in the center of the hearth. (F re: parlor of the Sartoris family)

Sartoris, 333:12

Tomorrow was **Christmas Eve** and the wagon was going into town . . . no word had been said to Bayard about his departure . . . (young Bayard at the MacCallum home)

Sartoris, 339:9

Rafe and the other boys would not be along for some time yet, what with **Christmas Eve** in town and the slow, festive gathering of the county. (young Bayard thinking about the MacCallum boys)

CHRISTMASTIDE

Sartoris, 60:9
... already in their minds the room was associated with death, an idea which even the holly and tinsel of **Christmastide** could not completely obscure. (F re: John and young Bayard)

CHURCH

Soldiers' Pay, 58:7
... from the Gothic mass of the **church** the spire rose, a prayer imperishable in bronze, immaculate in its illusion of slow ruin across motionless young clouds. (F)

Soldiers' Pay, 68:23
"How often has he appeared ... in **church,** at formal gatherings, carrying hat, coat and collar in his hands." (rector to Jones re: Donald Mahon)

Soldiers' Pay, 97:8
... his fellow townsmen ... looked askance at him because he and his family made periodical trips to Atlanta to attend **church.** (F re: Mr. Saunders)

Soldiers' Pay, 187:20
Mrs. Worthington ate too much and suffered from gout and a flouted will. So her **church** connection was rather trying to the minister and his flock. (F)

Soldiers' Pay, 231:2
"At our **church** they gave prizes for attendance and knowing the lesson, and my card bore forty-one stars, when it disappeared." (Jones to Mrs. Saunders)

Soldiers' Pay, 282:3
He conducted services in the dim oaken tunnel of the **church** while his flock hissed softly among themselves or slept between the responses... (F re: rector)

Soldiers' Pay, 313:14
The **church** loomed a black shadow with a silver roof ... (F)

Soldiers' Pay, 314:17
Jones doubled the **church** at a good speed and let himself out at the gate. (F)

Soldiers' Pay, 319:5
The singing drew nearer ... at last, crouching among a clump of trees beside the road, they saw the shabby **church** with its canting travesty of a spire. (rector and Joe Gilligan)

Soldiers' Pay, 319:27
They stood together in the dust, the rector in his shapeless black and Gilligan in his new hard serge, listening, seeing the shabby **church** become beautiful with mellow longing, passionate and sad. (F)

Mosquitoes, 36:1
"What did you think of my idea for getting a hundred percent **church** attendance by keeping them afraid they'd miss something good by staying away?" (Rotarian to Talliaferro)

Mosquitoes, 40:32
The Semitic man said: "My people produced Jesus, your people Christianized him. And ever since you have been trying to get him out of your **church**." (to Talliaferro et al)

Mosquitoes, 229:22
"Young people always shape their lives as the preceding generation requires of them. I don't mean that they go to **church** when they are told to, for instance, because their elders expect it of them . . ." (Semitic man to Fairchild)

Mosquitoes, 229:25
". . . though God only knows what other reason they could possibly have for going to **church** as it is conducted nowadays . . ." (Semitic man to Fairchild)

Mosquitoes, 229:29
". . . and all those traditional retreats that in the olden days enabled the **church** to produce a soul for every one it saved." (Semitic man to Fairchild)

Mosquitoes, 326:9
"I'd like to have seen her, coming out of the **church** afterward." (Semitic man to Fairchild re: Mrs. Maurier)

Sartoris, 24:12
Dat's whut de matter wid de **church** today. (Elnore)

Sartoris, 39:17
An effluvium of his primary calling clung about him always, however, even when he was swept and garnished for **church** and a little shapeless in a discarded Prince Albert coat of Bayard's . . . (F re: Simon)

Sartoris, 199:26
The duster and hat came down from the nail and the horses were harnessed to the carriage but once a week now—on Sundays, to drive in to town to **church**. (F re: Simon)

Sartoris, 199:28
Miss Jenny said she was too far along to jeopardize salvation by driving to **church** at fifty miles an hour . . . (F)

19

Sartoris, 232:20

"You see, dey been collectin' buildin' money fer dat **church** whut burnt down . . ." (Simon to old Bayard)

Sartoris, 232:22

". . . ez dey got de money up, dey turnt hit over ter me, whut wid my 'ficial position on de **church** boa'd en bein' I wuz a member of de bes' fambly round here." (Simon to old Bayard)

Sartoris, 272:19, 21

. . . "will you read out de total emoluments owed to de pupposed Secon' Baptis' **Church** by de late Deacon Strother in his capacity ez treasurer of de **church** boa'd?" (the leader to Brudder Mo')

Sartoris, 274:24, 25

"Deacon Strother," he said, "ez awdained minister of de late Fust Baptis' **Church,** en recalled minister of de pupposed Secon' Baptis' **Church** . . . " (the parson)

Sartoris, 274:28

"I hereby reinfests you wid yo' fawmer capacities of deacon in de said pupposed Secon' Baptis' **Church.**" (parson to Simon)

Sartoris, 275:4

But Simon was craning his head in the direction the **church** board had taken. (F)

Sartoris, 370:21

"The old grayheaded reprobate" . . . "So that's where that **church** money went that he 'put out.' " (Miss Jenny re: Simon)

Sartoris, 372:30

"I am not going to **church** today: I've been shut up between walls long enough." (Miss Jenny to Isom)

CHURCH CONFERENCE

Soldiers' Pay, 61:25

"Once I recall I was in a neighboring town attending a **conference.**" (rector to Jones)

Soldiers' Pay, 62:2

"So I left the bush uncovered against my better judgement and repaired to the **conference.**" (rector to Jones)

CHURCHES

Soldiers' Pay, 319:2

An occasional group of negroes passed them, bearing lighted lanterns that jetted vain little flames futilely into the moonlight. "No one knows why they do that . . . Perhaps it is to light their **churches** with." (rector to Joe Gilligan)

CHURCH SPIRE

Soldiers' Pay, 104:3
. . . pigeons about the **church spire** leaned upon it like silver and slanting splashes of soft paint. (F)

Soldiers' Pay, 114:29
They passed beneath the **church spire** and crossed the lawn. (rector and Mr. Saunders)

Soldiers' Pay, 116:10
The air was becoming sultry, oppressive; and the **church spire** had lost perspective until now it seemed but two dimensions of metal and cardboard. (F)

Soldiers' Pay, 170:2
. . . bees were humming golden arrows tipped or untipped with honey and from the **church spire** pigeons were remote and unemphatic as sleep. (F)

CIRCUMSTANCE

Soldiers' Pay, 155:14
"So you are meddling with Providence, are you?"
"Wouldn't you have done the same?" she defended herself.
"I never speculate on what I would have done," . . . "There can be no If in my profession. I work in tissue and bone, not in **circumstance**." (Dr. Baird and Mrs. Powers)

Soldiers' Pay, 317:20, 22
"**Circumstance** moves in marvellous ways, Joe."
"I thought you'd a said God, reverend."
"God is **circumstance**, Joe. God is in this life. We know nothing about the next. That will take care of itself in good time." (rector and Joe Gilligan)

CLERGY

Soldiers' Pay, 289:7
"That's what association with the **clergy** does for you," he said crassly. (Jones to rector)

Mosquitoes, 219:16
"But during the Great Fire all the registrars' and parsons' homes were destroyed . . . In the meantime quite a few young people had gone there in all sincerity, you know, and were forced to return the next day without benefit of **clergy**." (Major Ayers to Fairchild et al)

Sartoris, 74:28
"At least, give me benefit of **clergy** first, Aunt Sally," Narcissa said.

21

CLERICAL CLOTH

Soldiers' Pay, 57:5
"But one of my **cloth** is prone to allow his own soul to atrophy in his zeal for the welfare of other souls . . ." (rector to Jones)

Soldiers' Pay, 57:20
"There are certain conventions which we must observe in this world: one of them being an outward deference to that **cloth** which I unworthily, perhaps, wear." (rector to Jones)

Soldiers' Pay, 60:24
"I thought we had declared a truce regarding each other's **cloth**." (Jones to rector)

Soldiers' Pay, 60:27
"What is your **cloth**?" (rector to Jones)

Soldiers' Pay, 66:10
The rector assailed him with ruthless kindness and the gingham-clad one reappeared at the door with a twin of the rector's casual **black nether coverings** over her arm. (rector, Jones and Emmy)

Soldiers' Pay, 82:3
She turned graceful as a flower stalk against the rector's **black bulk**. (Cecily)

Soldiers' Pay, 180:32
She crossed grass and the rector rose, huge as a rock, **black and shapeless**, greeting her. (Mrs. Burney)

Soldiers' Pay, 181:28
Pigeons like slow sleep, afternoon passing away, dying. Mrs. Burney, in her tight, hot black, the rector, huge and **black and shapeless** . . . (F)

Soldiers' Pay, 256:22
He paused mountainous and **shapeless** in his casual **black** . . . (rector)

Soldiers' Pay, 319:25
They stood together in the dust, the rector in **shapeless black**, and Gilligan in his new hard serge, listening, seeing the shabby church become beautiful . . . (F)

CLOISTER

Soldiers' Pay, 61:13
Against a privot hedge would soon be lilies like nuns in a **cloister** and blue hyacinths swung soundless bells, dreaming of Lesbos. (F)

22

CLOISTERED

Mosquitoes, 230:10, 12

"A few years ago a so called commercial artist . . . named John Held began to caricature college life, **cloistered** and otherwise, in the magazines; ever since then college life, **cloistered** and otherwise, has been busy caricaturing John Held." (Semitic man to Fairchild)

COMPASSIONATE

Soldiers' Pay, 58:23

"Our God . . . need not be **compassionate,** he need not be very intelligent. But he must have dignity." (Jones to rector)

CONVICTION

Mosquitoes, 184:6

"Dawson clings to his **conviction** for the old reason: it's good enough to live with and comfortable to die with—like a belief in immortality." (Mrs. Wiseman to Semitic man et al)

CONVICTIONS

Mosquitoes, 40:25

"And **convictions** are always alarming, unless you are looking at them from behind." (Fairchild to Semitic man et al)

Mosquitoes, 131:6

"After all, it doesn't make any difference what you believe. Man is not only nourished by **convictions,** he is nourished by any conviction. Whatever you believe, you'll always annoy some one, but you yourself will follow and bleed and die for it in the face of law, hell or high water." (Semitic man to Fairchild)

Sartoris, 9:33

. . . he believed too firmly in Providence, as all his actions clearly showed, to have any religious **convictions** whatever. (F re: Bayard Sartoris of Carolina)

COSMIC SCHEME

Soldiers' Pay, 283:31

He had failed twice: this time success must be his or the whole **cosmic scheme** would crumble, hurling him, screaming, into blackness, where no blackness was, death where death was not. (F re: Jones)

Mosquitoes, 131:18

" . . . were it not Mussolini and his illusion it would be some one else and his cause. I believe it is some grand **cosmic scheme** for fertilizing the earth." (Semitic man to Fairchild)

CREATE

Mosquitoes, 320:14

"But in art, a man can **create** without any assistance at all: what he does is his." (Fairchild to Semitic man)

Mosquitoes, 339:10

Dante invented Beatrice . . . a maid that life had not had time to **create,** and laid upon her frail and unbowed shoulders the whole burden of man's history . . . (F)

CREATED

Soldiers' Pay, 314:32

Male and female **created** He them, young. (F)

CREATING

Soldiers' Pay, 59:25

He rather wished the rector . . . had had the **creating** of things and that he, Jones, could be forever thirty-one years of age.

Mosquitoes, 339:9

Dante invented Beatrice, **creating** himself a maid . . . (F)

CREATION

Mosquitoes, 320:18

"**Creation,** reproduction from within . . . Is the dominating impulse in the world feminine, after all, as aboriginal peoples believe?" (Fairchild to Semitic man)

CREATOR

Soldiers' Pay, 64:2

"Even that part of the body which the **Creator** designed for sitting on serves him only a short time, then it rebels, then it, too, gets his sullen bones up and hales them along." (rector to Jones)

CROSS

Soldiers' Pay, 56:16

His shining dome was friendly against an ivy-covered wall above which the consummate grace of a spire and a gilded **cross** seemed to arc across motionless young clouds. (F re: rector)

Mosquitoes, 340:12

The priests **cross** themselves while the nuns of silence blend anew their breath, and pass on . . . (F)

CROSS MOTIF

Soldiers' Pay, 60:31

His arm was heavy and solid as an **oak branch** across Jones' shoulder. (F re: rector)

Soldiers' Pay, 83:1

The rector fetched his photograph . . . and that girl leaning against the **oaken branch** of the rector's arm, believing that she is in love with the boy, or his illusion—pretending she is, anyway. (rector, Cecily, and Donald)

CRUCIFIXION MOTIF

Soldiers' Pay, 35:23

But this was soon lost in the mellow death of evening in a street between stone buildings, among lights, and Gilligan in his awkward khaki and the girl in her rough coat, **holding each an arm of Donald Mahon,** silhouetted against it in the doorway. (F)

Soldiers' Pay, 312:24

After a while passing beneath **crossed skeletoned arms** on a pole he crossed the railroad and followed a lane between negro cabins . . . (F re: Gilligan)

Mosquitoes, 211:30

She stood beside a cypress, up to her knees in thick water, **her arms crossed** against the tree trunk and her face hidden in her arms, utterly motionless. (F re: Patricia in the swamp)

CRUSADE

Mosquitoes, 41:7

"The only ones who ever gain by the spiritual machinations of mankind are the small minority who gain emotional or mental or physical exercise from the activity itself, never the passive majority for whom the **crusade** is set afoot." (Semitic man to Talliaferro)

CRUSADING

Sartoris, 9:26

His high-colored face wore an expression of frank and high-hearted dullness which you imagine Richard First as wearing before he went **crusading** . . . (F re: Bayard Sartoris of Carolina)

CURSE[1]

Soldiers' Pay, 60:7

"And that is already the **curse** of our civilization—Things, Possessions, to which we are slaves, which require us to either labor honestly . . . or do something illegal so as to keep them painted or dressed in the latest mode or filled with whisky or gasoline." (Jones to rector)

---

1 See also Appendix A, p. 129.

CURSED

Mosquitoes, 41:33

"I have no quarrel with education. I don't think it hurts you much, except to make you unhappy and unfit for work, for which man was **cursed** by the gods before they had learned about education." (Semitic man to Fairchild)

Mosquitoes, 47:3, 3

fool fool you have work to do o **cursed** of god **cursed** and forgotten ... (Gordon)

Mosquitoes, 48:16

. . . fool fool **cursed** and forgotten of god (Gordon)

Mosquitoes, 171:19

A huge gaudy bird came up and **cursed** her, and the snake ignored her with a sort of tired unillusion and plopped heavily into the thick water. (F re: Patricia in the swamp)

CURSING

Mosquitoes, 180:13

The road went on shimmering before them, endless beneath bearded watching trees, crossing the implacable swamp with a puerile bravado like a thin voice **cursing** in a cathedral. (F re: David and Patricia in the swamp)

CYPRESS TREES

Mosquitoes, 82:31

. . . the Nausikaa at half speed forged slowly into a sluggish river mouth, broaching a timeless violet twilight between solemn bearded **cypresses** motionless as bronze. (F)

Mosquitoes, 83:4

The world was becoming dimensionless, the tall bearded **cypresses** drew nearer one to another across the wallowing river with the soulless implacability of pagan gods, gazing down upon this mahogany-and-brass intruder with inscrutable unalarm. (F)

Mosquitoes, 169:19

Trees heavy and ancient with moss loomed out of it hugely and grayly: the mist might have been a sluggish growth between and among them. (F)

Mosquitoes, 169:24

. . . these huge and silent **trees** might have been the first of living things, too recently born to know either fear or astonishment, dragging their sluggish umbilical cords from out the old miasmic womb of a nothingness latent and dreadful. (F)

Mosquitoes, 171:3, 4

The mist broke raggedly and drifted in sluggish wraiths that seemed to devour all sound, swaying and swinging like huge spectral apes from **tree** to **tree,** rising and falling, revealing somber patriarchs of **trees,** hiding them again. (F)

Mosquitoes, 172:15

The mist had gone, and the sun came already sinister and hot among the **trees,** upon the miasmic earth. (F)

Mosquitoes, 174:5

Huge **cypress** roots thrust up like weathered bones out of a green scum and a quaking neither earth nor water . . . (F)

Mosquitoes, 174:8

. . . always those bearded eternal **trees** like gods regarding without alarm this puny desecration of a silence of air and earth and water ancient when hoary old Time himself was a pink and dreadful miracle in his mother's arms. (F)

Mosquitoes, 174:15

It was she who found the fallen tree, who first essayed its oozy treacherous bark and first stood in the empty road stretching monotonously in either direction between battalioned patriarchs of **trees.** (F re: Patricia)

Mosquitoes, 180:12

The road went on shimmering before them, endless beneath bearded watching **trees,** crossing the implacable swamp with a puerile bravado like a thin voice cursing in a cathedral. (F re: David and Patricia)

Mosquitoes, 187:15

Beside them always and always those eternal bearded **trees,** bearded and brooding, older and stiller than eternity. (F re: David and Patricia)

Mosquitoes, 205:4

Trees without tops passed him, marched up abreast of him, topless, and fell behind; the rank roadside grass approached and became monstrous and separate, blade by blade . . . (F re: David)

Mosquitoes, 211:25

The road had dropped downward again into the swamp where amid rank, impenetrable jungle dark streams wallowed aimless and obscene, and against the hidden flame of the west huge **trees** brooded bearded and ancient as prophets out of Genesis. (F)

Mosquitoes, 211:29, 30

She stood beside a **cypress,** up to her knees in thick water, her arms crossed against the **tree** trunk and her face hidden in her arms, utterly motionless. (F re: Patricia)

27

Mosquitoes, 213:15
Then the sound came again across the afternoon, among the patriarchal **trees**—a faint, fretful sound. (F)

DAMNATION[1]

Soldiers' Pay, 178:24
Gas. Bullets and death and **damnation**. But Gas. It looked like mist,
they had been told. First thing you know you are in it. And then
—Good-night. (F re: soldiers in battle)

Soldiers' Pay, 319:30
Then the singing died, fading away along the mooned land inevitable
with tomorrow and sweat, with sex and death and **damnation;** and
they turned townward under the moon, feeling dust in their shoes.
(F re: rector and Joe Gilligan)

DANTE

Mosquitoes, 339:8
Dante invented Beatrice creating himself a maid that life had not
had time to create, and laid upon her frail and unbowed shoulders
the whole burden of man's history. . . . (F)

DAVID

Mosquitoes, passim
David West, steward on Mrs. Maurier's yacht

DEACON

Sartoris, passim
Deacon, proprietor at a restaurant-store in Jefferson

Sartoris, passim
Deacon Simon Strother of the Baptis' Church and servant of the
Sartoris family

DEITY

Sartoris, 23:21
And the next day he was dead . . . by losing the frustration of his
own flesh he could now stiffen and shape that which sprang from
him into the fatal semblance of his dream; to be evoked like a genie
or a **deity** by an illiterate old man's tedious reminiscing . . . (F re:
Colonel John Sartoris)

---

1 See also Appendix A, p. 129.

DELILAH

Sartoris, 204:30

He had been so neatly tricked by earth, that ancient **Deliah,** that he was not aware that his locks were shorn . . . (F re: young Bayard)

DEMONIAC

Mosquitoes, 80:16

Fairchild looked more like a walrus than ever: a deceptively sedate walrus of middle age suddenly evincing a streak of **demoniac** puerility. (F)

DENOMINATIONAL

Mosquitoes, 115:21

"It was a kind of funny college I went to. A **denominational** college, you know, where they turn out preachers." (Fairchild to Josh)

DERVISH

Soldiers' Pay, 278:16

The Baptist minister, a young **dervish** in a white lawn tie, being most available, came and did his duty and went away. (F)

Soldiers' Pay, 295:11

(First, marched a uniformed self-constituted guard . . . and a Boy Scout bugler furnished by the young Baptist minister, a fiery-eyed **dervish,** who had served in the Y.M.C.A.) (F)

Soldiers' Pay, 298:7

(The sun had gone, had been recalled as quickly as a usurer's note and the doves fell silent and went away. The Baptist **dervish's** Boy Scout lipped his bugle, sounding taps.) (F)

DESOLATION

Mosquitoes, 127:12

. . . that surge of imminence and fire and **desolation** . . . (F re: Talliaferro)

DESTINY

Soldiers' Pay, 311:11

He too knew a sense of freedom, of being master of his **destiny.** (F re: Joe Gilligan)

Sartoris, 92:27

Fatality; the augury of a man's **destiny** peeping out at him from the roadside hedge . . . (F re: old Bayard)

Sartoris, 93:8

The upturned corners of man's **destiny**. Well, heaven, that crowded place . . . heaven filled with every man's illusion of himself and with the conflicting illusions of him that parade through the minds of other illusions . . . (F re: old Bayard)

Sartoris, 351:17

. . . for the time being he had quitted the desk and the room and the town and all the crude and blatant newness into which his **destiny** had brought him . . . (F re: Horace)

DEVIL

Soldiers' Pay, 223:7

"It would be a **devil** of a chaotic world if you never could count on whether or not people mean what they say." (Jones to Cecily)

Soldiers' Pay, 248:28

"You can never tell just exactly how dead these soldiers are, can you? You think you have him and then the **devil** reveals as much idiocy as a normal sane person doesn't he?" (Jones to Mrs. Powers)

Mosquitoes, 116:7

". . . one instructor always insisted that the head **devil** in *Paradise Lost* was an inspired prophetic portrait of Darwin . . ." (Fairchild to Josh)

Sartoris, 56:17

"Bayard love anybody, that cold **devil**?" (Miss Jenny to Narcissa)

Sartoris, 85:7

"Ask, the **devil**," Miss Jenny said. (to old Bayard)

Sartoris, 362:20

"Say, you remember that night in Amiens when that big Irish **devil**, Comyn, wrecked the Cloche-Clos by blowing that A.P.M.'s whistle at the door?" (aviator to young Bayard)

DEVILMENT

Sartoris, 200:14

"Mark my words . . . he's storing up **devilment** that's going to burst loose all at once, some day." (Miss Jenny to Narcissa re: young Bayard)

DEVOTION

Soldiers' Pay, 268:14

George Farr had been quite drunk for a week. . . . even the town soaks began to look upon him with respect, calling him by his given name, swearing undying **devotion** to him. (F)

30

DIABOLIC

Soldiers' Pay, 217:4

The man was a nemesis . . . he had flouted her, had injured her with **diabolic** ingenuity. (Cecily re: Jones)

DIABOLICAL

Soldiers' Pay, 20:12

They half dragged, half carried the two civilians and with **diabolical** cunning Yaphank led the way through the train and dismounted from a day coach. (F)

DIVINE (NOMENCLATURE)

Soldiers' Pay, 58:10

"My one sincere parishioner," murmered the **divine**. (rector to Jones)

Soldiers' Pay, 115:20

. . . he and the **divine** followed her up the stairs. (Mr. Saunders, rector and Mrs. Powers)

Soldiers' Pay, 255:28

The **divine** made a clicking sound. "This is bad. I had not expected this." (rector to Mr. Saunders)

Soldiers' Pay, 287:11

"Running?" the **divine** repeated. (rector to Jones)

Soldiers' Pay, 318:1

The **divine** put his heavy arm across Gilligan's shoulder. . . . "The saddest thing about love, Joe, is that not only love cannot last forever, but even heartbreak is soon forgotten." (rector to Gilligan)

Soldiers' Pay, 318:23

Beyond it an orchard slept the night away in symmetrical rows, squatting and pregnant. "Willard has good fruit," the **divine** murmured. (rector to Joe Gilligan)

Soldiers' Pay, 319:1

An occasional group of negroes passed them, bearing lighted lanterns that jetted vain little flames futilely into the moonlight. "No one knows why they do that," the **divine** replied to Gilligan's question. "Perhaps it is to light their churches with." (rector)

DIVINE PROVIDENCE

Sartoris, 74:18

"Even Lucy Cranston, come of as good people as there are in the state, acting like it was **divine providence** that let her marry one Sartoris and be the mother of two more. Pride, false pride." (Aunt Sally to Narcissa)

DIVINITY ALLUSIONS

Soldiers' Pay, 111:16
(. . . if the Lord had intended folks to fly around in the air **He'd 'a'** give 'em wings.) (townspeople)

Soldiers' Pay, 297:24, 29
(I am the Resurrection and the Life, saith the Lord . . .) . . .
(Whosoever believeth in **Me**, though he were dead . . .) . . .
(. . . yet shall he live. And whosoever liveth and believeth in **Me** shall never die . . .) (F)

Soldiers' Pay, 314:32
Male and female created **He** them, young. (F)

Soldiers' Pay, 319:12
It was nothing, it was everything; then it swelled to an ecstasy, taking the white man's words as readily as it took his remote God and made a personal Father of **Him**. (F re: Negroes singing)

Mosquitoes, 40:19
"God must look upon our American scene with a good deal of consternation, watching the antics of these volunteers who are trying to help **Him**." (Fairchild to Semitic man et al)

Mosquitoes, 328:2
"Prohibition for the Latin, politics for the Irish, invented **He** them." (Semitic man to Fairchild et al)

Mosquitoes, 328:6
"Where do we home Nordics come in? What has **He** invented for us?" (Fairchild to Semitic man et al)

Sartoris, 66:23, 24
"De good Lawd took keer of you fer a long time, now, but **He** ain't gwine bother wid you always." (Simon)
"Den I reckon I'll git along widout **Him**," Caspey retorted.

Sartoris, 150:19
"Ef de Lawd don't take no better keer of me dan **He** done of dat hat, I don't wanter go dar, noways," . . . (first Negro to second Negro)

Sartoris, 296:20, 20
. . . Simon stood overlooking the field somewhat as . . . the Lord God **Himself** when **He** contemplated his latest chemical experiment and saw that it was good. (F)

Sartoris, 374:17
'I bare him on eagles' wings
and brought him unto **Me'**   (epitaph for Lieutenant John Sartoris)

Sartoris, 379:23

"I reckon the Lord knows **His** business, but I declare, sometimes . . . Play something." (Miss Jenny to Narcissa)

Sartoris, 380:17, 18, 18, 18

But the **Player,** and the game **He** plays . . . **He** must have a name for **His** pawns, though. (F)

Sartoris, 380:22

But perhaps Sartoris is the game itself—a game outmoded and played with pawns shaped too late and to an old dead pattern, and of which the **Player Himself** is a little wearied. (F)

DOCTRINE

Soldiers' Pay, 249:3

"It seems to me that is a rather precarious **doctrine** for one who is— if you will pardon me—not exactly a combative sort." (Mrs. Powers to Jones)

Soldiers' Pay, 317:26

"Ain't that a kind of funny **doctrine** for a parson to get off?" (Joe Gilligan to rector)

DOGMA

Mosquitoes, 116:4

"There were a bunch of brokendown preachers: head full of **dogma** and intolerance . . ." (Fairchild to Josh)

DOOM

Sartoris, 23:7

It showed on John Sartoris' brow, the dark shadow of fatality and **doom,** that night when he sat beneath the candles in the dining-room and turned a wineglass in his fingers while he talked to his son. (F)

Sartoris, 23:11

The railroad was finished, and that day he had been elected to the state legislature after a hard and bitter fight, and **doom** lay on his brow, and weariness. (F re: Colonel John Sartoris)

Sartoris, 107:30

. . . the fowls themselves, perhaps with a foreknowledge of frustration and of **doom,** huddled back and forth along the wire, discordant and distracted . . . (F)

Sartoris, 126:14

. . . he fell to talking of the war. Not of combat, but rather of a life peopled by young men like fallen angels, and of a meteoric violence like that of fallen angels, beyond heaven or hell and partaking of both: doomed immortality and immortal **doom.** (young Bayard)

Sartoris, 289:22
She took his face between her palms and drew it down, but his lips were cold and upon them she tasted fatality and **doom,** and she clung to him for a time . . . (Narcissa and young Bayard)

Sartoris, 289:32
And they would lie so, holding one another in the darkness and the temporary abeyance of his despair and the isolation of that **doom** he could not escape. (Narcissa and young Bayard)

Sartoris, 312:24
But he remembered that unmistakable feel of his grandfather when he had touched him . . . so erect and firm for so long by pride and the perverse necessity of his family **doom,** had given away all at once, letting his skeleton rest at last. (young Bayard)

Sartoris, 354:14
Miss Jenny felt that old Bayard had somehow flouted them all, had committed lese majesty toward his ancestors and the lusty glamour of the family **doom** by dying . . . practically from the "inside out." (F)

Sartoris, 356:15
. . . it was as though already she could discern the dark shape of that **doom** which she had incurred, standing beside her chair, waiting and biding its time. (F re: Narcissa)

Sartoris, 357:33
. . . a period at which the men themselves, for all their headlong and scornful rashness, would have quailed had their parts been passive parts and their **doom** been waiting. (F)

DOOMED

Sartoris, 126:13
. . . he fell to talking of the war. Not of combat, but rather of a life peopled by young men like fallen angels . . . beyond heaven or hell and partaking of both: **doomed** immortality and immortal doom. (young Bayard)

DOVES

Soldiers' Pay, 297:13
Away, following where fingers of sunlight pointed among cedars, **doves** were cool, throatily unemphatic among the dead. (F re: the cemetery)

34

Soldiers' Pay, 298:6

The sun had gone, had been recalled as quick as a usurer's note and the **doves** fell silent or went away. (F)

Mosquitoes, 64:19

"The American flag and a couple of **doves** holding dollar marks in their bills ..." (Fairchild to Josh et al)

Sartoris, 180:2

Then Horace was in school at Sewanee and later at Oxford, from which he returned just in time to see Will Benbow join his wife among pointed cedars and carven **doves** and other serene marble shapes ... (F)

Sartoris, 373:19, 22

Now and then they were surmounted by symbolical urns and **doves** and surrounded by clipped, tended sward green against the blanched marble and the blue dappled sky and the black cedars from amid which **doves** crooned, endlessly reiterant. (F re: Miss Jenny and Isom in the cemetery)

Sartoris, 374:20

Across the spaced tranquillity of the marble shapes the **doves** crooned their endless rising inflections. (F re: the cemetery)

Sartoris, 376:8

The wind drew among the cedars in long sighs, and steadily as pulses the sad hopeless reiteration of the **doves** came along the sunny air. (F)

DRUID PRIEST

Mosquitoes, 92:4

"You simply cannot tell what they're going to do," she said ... seeing again Major Ayers' vanishing awkward shape and Fairchild leaning over the rail and howling after him like a bullvoiced **Druid priest** at a sacrifice. (Mrs. Maurier to Mrs. Wiseman et al)

EAGLE

Mosquitoes, 26:21

"The untrammeled spirit, freedom like the **eagle's**." (Mrs. Maurier to Talliaferro et al)

Sartoris, 375:10

... beneath which the headstones of the wives whom they had dragged into their arrogant orbits were, despite their pompous genealogical references, modest and effacing as the song of the thrushes beneath the eyrie of an **eagle**. (F re: wives of the Sartoris family)

EAGLES' WINGS

Sartoris, 374:16

'I bare him on **eagles' wings**
and brought him unto Me'   (epitaph of Lieutenant John Sartoris)

EPISCOPAL

Soldiers' Pay, 261:17

Funny goings-on in that house. And a preacher of the gospel, too.
Even is he is **Episcopal.** If he wasn't such a nice man . . . (voices in
the town re: rector)

Soldiers' Pay, 278:22

. . . he liked and respected Dr. Mahon, refusing to believe that
simply because Dr. Mahon was **Episcopal** he was going to hell as
soon as he died. (F re: Baptist minister and rector)

ETERNAL

Soldiers' Pay, 112:28

They passed beneath a stone shaft bearing a Confederate soldier
shading his marble eyes forever in **eternal** rigid vigilance . . . (F re:
Mr. Saunders and rector)

Soldiers' Pay, 176:23

He thought at times of Captain Green as he crossed France, seeing
the intermittent silver smugness of rain spaced forever with poplars
like an **eternal** frieze giving way upon vistas fallow and fecund . . .
(Sergeant Madden)

Mosquitoes, 11:5

What this room troubled was something **eternal** in the race, something immortal. (F)

Mosquitoes, 11:25

. . . you got again untarnished and high and clean that sense of
swiftness, of space encompassed; but on looking again it was as
before: motionless and passionately **eternal** . . . (F re: a statue)

Mosquitoes, 11:28

. . . marble temporarily caught and hushed yet passionate still for
escape, passionate and simple and **eternal** in the equivocal derisive
darkness of the world. (F re: a statue)

Mosquitoes, 42:4

"But to go back to religion"—"the spirit protestant **eternal**," . . .
(blond young man to Fairchild et al)

Mosquitoes, 151:15

The moon was getting up and Pete's straw hat was a dull implacable
gleam slanted above the red eye of the **eternal** cigarette. (F)

Mosquitoes, 174:8

. . . always those bearded **eternal** trees like gods . . . (F)

Mosquitoes, 187:15

Besides them always and always those **eternal** bearded trees, bearded and brooding, older and stiller than eternity. (F re: David and Patricia)

Mosquitoes, 243:12

For by getting himself and his own bewilderment and inhibitations out of the way by describing . . . American life as American life is, it will become **eternal** and timeless despite him. (Julius to Mark Frost et al)

Mosquitoes, 274:20

The others were seated and well into their dinner, but before four vacant places that bland **eternal** grapefruit, sinister and bland as taxes. (F)

Mosquitoes, 336:29

About him the city swooned in a voluption of dark and heat, a sleep which was not sleep; and dark and heat lapped his burly short body about with the hidden **eternal** pulse of the world. (F re: Semitic man)

Mosquitoes, 339:5

Then voices and sounds, shadows and echoes change form swirling, becoming the headless, armless, legless torso of a girl, motionless and virginal and passionately **eternal** before the shadows and echoes swirl away. (F)

Sartoris, 297:19

. . . only a lone hickory at the foot of the park kept its leaves, gleaming like a sodden flame on the **eternal** azure, and beyond the valley the hills were hidden by a swaddling of rain. (F)

ETERNALLY

Soldiers' Pay, 67:23

"There is always death in the faces of the young in spirit, the **eternally** young. Death for themselves or for others." (rector to Jones)

Sartoris, 272:1

"I'll be **eternally** damned if I will; if I let a lazy nigger that ain't worth his keep—" (old Bayard to Simon)

ETERNITY

Soldiers' Pay, 99:31

The oaks on the lawn became still with dusk, and the branches of trees were as motionless as coral fathoms deep under seas. A tree frog took up his monotonous trilling and the west was a vast green lake, still as **eternity**. (F)

Mosquitoes, 11:14
. . . shades of servants and masters now in a more gracious region, lending dignity to **eternity.** (F)

Mosquitoes, 53:1
". . . I've got to pass the time in some way in order to gain some idea of how to pass **eternity,**" the Semitic man answered. (to Fairchild)

Mosquitoes, 187:16
Beside them always and always those eternal bearded trees . . . older and stiller than **eternity.** (F re: David and Patricia)

EVE (EVA)

Mosquitoes, passim
Eva Wiseman, sister of the Semitic man and guest on Mrs. Maurier's yacht

EVIL

Mosquitoes, 31:17
But Mrs. Maurier's fingers were but leaving his cheeks and the niece was invisible in her corner: a bodiless **evil.** (Talliaferro)

Mosquitoes, 228:23
". . . she went off with Da—the Steward. It was kind of nice, wasn't it? And came back. No excuses, no explanations—'think no **evil**' you know." (Fairchild to Semitic man et al)

Mosquitoes, 228:25
"Only old folks like Julius and me would ever see **evil** in what people, young people do." (Fairchild to Semitic man et al)

Mosquitoes, 228:27
"But then, I guess folks growing up into the manner of looking at life that we inherited, would find **evil** in anything where inclination wasn't subservient to duty." (Fairchild to Semitic man et al)

Sartoris, 42:15
Simon had fired his cigar at last, and the **evil** smoke of it trailed behind him, fading. (F)

EVIL JUDGMENT

Sartoris, 115:31
At the door and with one foot raised to the running-board, he made a final stand against the subtle powers of **evil judgment.** (Simon)

EXODUS

Soldiers' Pay, 233:25
George Farr, lurking along a street, climbed a fence swiftly when the **exodus** from the picture show came along. (F)

Soldiers' Pay, 234:2

So he gave up and became frankly skulking, climbing a fence smartly when the **exodus** from the picture show began. (George Farr)

EXPIATING

Sartoris, 229:15

"I'll declare, sometimes I just lose patience with you folks; wonder what crime I seem to be **expiating** by having to live with you." (Miss Jenny to old Bayard)

FAITH

Mosquitoes, 32:31

Here he felt that he had at last come into his own . . . and his restored **faith** in himself enabled him to rise with comfortable ease to the coveted position of wholesale buyer. (Talliaferro)

Mosquitoes, 42:21

"It seems to me that the Protestant **faith** was invented for the sole purpose of filling our jails and morgues and houses of detention." (Semitic man to Fairchild)

Mosquitoes, 130:29

"And more than that, think what a devil of a fix you and I'd be in were it not for words, were we to lose our **faith** in words." (Semitic man to Fairchild)

FAITH, HOPE AND CHARITY

Sartoris, 279:2

Outcast and pariah, he has neither friend, wife, mistress, nor sweetheart; celibate, he is unscarred, possesses neither pillar nor desert cave, he is not assaulted by temptations nor flagellated by dreams nor assuaged by vision; **faith, hope and charity** are not his. (F re: the mule)

FATALITY

Sartoris, 23:7

It showed on John Sartoris' brow, the dark shadow of **fatality** and doom, that night when he sat beneath the candles in the dining-room and turned a wineglass in his fingers while he talked to his son. (F)

Sartoris, 92:27

Fatality, the augury of a man's destiny peeping out at him from the roadside hedge . . . (F)

Sartoris, 380:23

For there is death in the sound of it, and a glamorous **fatality,** like silver pennons downrushing at sunset, or a dying fall of horns along the road to Roncevaux. (F)

FATE

Soldiers' Pay, 27:15
He was deftly officious, including them impartially in his activities, like **Fate**. (porter on train)

Soldiers' Pay, 29:19
"What do you mean, Chateau Thierry?" said Lowe, boyish in disappointment, feeling that he had been deliberately ignored by one to whom **Fate** had been kinder than to himself. (to Gilligan)

Soldiers' Pay, 36:7
She thought of her husband youngly dead in France in a recurrence of fretful exasperation with having been tricked by a wanton **Fate**: a joke amusing to no one. (Mrs. Powers)

Soldiers' Pay, 52:33
He saw a tomb, open, and himself in boots and belt, and pilot's wings on his breast, a wound stripe . . . What more could one ask of **Fate?** (Lowe)

Soldiers' Pay, 70:30
The rector was saying bland as **Fate**: "I had expected you earlier." (to Cecily)

Soldiers' Pay, 174:4
But **Fate**, using the War Department as an instrument, circumvented them. (F re: soldiers)

Soldiers' Pay, 180:9
. . . above her dull and quenchless sorrow she knew a faint pride: the stroke of **Fate** which robbed her likewise made of her an aristocrat. (Mrs. Burney re: death of her son)

Soldiers' Pay, 242:24
Even **Fate** envied him this happiness, this unbearable happiness, he thought bitterly. (George Farr)

Mosquitoes, 8:13
. . . the majesty of **Fate** became contemptuous through ubiquity and sheer repetition. (F)

FATEFUL

Sartoris, 273:30
The parson, however, still retained his former attitude of **fateful** and impressive profundity. (F)

Sartoris, 375:16
His head was lifted a little in that gesture of haughty pride which repeated itself generation after generation with a **fateful** fidelity . . . (F re: statue of Colonel John Sartoris)

40

FATES

Mosquitoes, 307:22

The two dark windows were inscrutable as two **fates.** He pressed the bell, then stepped back to complete his aria. (Talliaferro)

FATHER (GOD)

Soldiers' Pay, 319:12

It was nothing, it was everything; then it swelled to an ecstasy, taking the white man's words as readily as it took his remote God and made a personal **Father** of Him. (F re: Negroes singing)

FIENDISH

Sartoris, 204:8

. . . he no longer took cold and **fiendish** pleasure in turning curves on two wheels or detaching mules from wagons by striking the whiffletrees with his bumper in passing. (F re: young Bayard)

FLOCK (CHURCH)

Soldiers' Pay, 187:21

Mrs. Worthington ate too much and suffered from gout and a flouted will. So her church connection was rather trying to the minister and his **flock.** (F)

Soldiers' Pay, 282:3

He conducted services in the dim oaken tunnel of the church while his **flock** hissed softly among themselves or slept between the responses, while pigeons held their own crooning rituals of audible slumber in the spire . . . (F re: rector)

GABRIEL (EXPLETIVE ONLY)

Mosquitoes

Gabriel used by Patricia and Josh Robyn
59:19, 77:5, 86:9, 135:4, 138:12, 143:22, 243:26,
244:17, 244:19, 270:19, 270:20

GARLANDED

Sartoris, 61:5

. . . Jeb Stuart himself, perhaps, on his glittering **garlanded** bay or with his sunny hair falling upon fine broadcloth beneath the mistletoe and holly boughs of Baltimore in '58 (F)

GAT (BEGAT)

Mosquitoes, 47:6

. . . shapes out of chaos more satisfactory than bread to the belly form by a madmans dream **gat** on the body of chaos . . . (Gordon)

41

GENESIS

Mosquitoes, 211:26
. . . against the hidden flame of the west huge trees brooded bearded and ancient as prophets out of **Genesis**. (F)

GETHSEMANE

Mosquitoes, 48:1
stars in my hair in my hair and beard i am crowned with stars christ by his own hand an auto**gethsemane** carved darkly out of pure space . . . (Gordon)

GHOST

Soldiers' Pay, 148:4
He felt nothing, yet like an unattached **ghost** he felt compelled to linger around the corner . . . (George Farr)

Soldiers' Pay, 165:14
Night was almost come: only the footprint of day, only the odor of day, only a rumor, a **ghost** of light among the trees. (F)

Soldiers' Pay, 224:32
"If I really held you close you'd pass right through me like a **ghost,** I am afraid," . . . (Jones to Cecily)

Mosquitoes, 164:17
Up from the darkness of the companionway the niece came, naked and silent as a **ghost**. (F re: Patricia)

Mosquitoes, 225:22
Here was a vague **ghost** of the scent she liked . . . (Jenny)

Mosquitoes, 233:29
"But all you have of it now is a kind of **ghost** of happiness and a vague and meaningless regret." (Fairchild to Semitic man)

Mosquitoes, 265:28
"Are you a **ghost**, or am I?" (Fairchild to Gordon)

Mosquitoes, 326:32
"But now her body is old; it no longer remembers that it missed anything, and all she has left is a habit, the **ghost** of a need to rectify something . . . (Fairchild to Semitic man re: Mrs. Maurier)

Sartoris, 31:30
"I've lived with these bullheaded Sartorises for eighty years, and I'll never give a single **ghost** of 'em the satisfaction of shedding a tear over him." (Miss Jenny to Narcissa re: John)

Sartoris, 259:6

. . . they talked, quietly and impersonally, with the **ghost** of that other afternoon between them though neither ever referred to it. (young Bayard and Narcissa)

Sartoris, 297:28

. . . in the yellow firelight of their room she would cling to him, or lie crying quietly in the darkness beside his rigid body, with a **ghost** between them. (young Bayard and Narcissa)

GHOSTLINESS

Mosquitoes, 330:22

His very **ghostliness** seemed to annihilate space: he invariably arrived after you had forgotten about him and before you expected him. (F re: Mark Frost)

Sartoris, 257:20

Just before he slept, his mind, with the mind's uncanny attribute for irrelevant recapitulation, reproduced with the startling **ghostliness** of a dictaphone an incident which at the time he had considered trivial. (Horace)

GHOSTLY

Soldiers' Pay, 25:8

Occasional trees and houses marching through it; and towns like bubbles of **ghostly** sound beaded on a steel wire— (F)

Mosquitoes, 34:18

. . . then his glance took in . . . a tall, **ghostly** young man with a thin evaporation of fair hair and a pale prehensile mouth . . . (F re: Talliaferro and Mark Frost)

Mosquitoes, 83:27

At the companionway the **ghostly** poet joined them hurriedly, flapping his handkerchief about his face and neck and the top of his unnurtured evaporating head. (F re: Mark Frost)

Mosquitoes, 84:22

"I'm the best poet in New Orleans," the **ghostly** young man said heavily, mooning his pale prehensile face at her. (Mark Frost to Mrs. Wiseman)

Mosquitoes, 88:18

"Why doesn't he establish a European agent?" the **ghostly** poet added viciously. (Mark Frost to Fairchild et al)

Mosquitoes, 95:9

The **ghostly** poet rose obediently and Mrs. Wiseman swept her hand amid the cards on the table, scattering them. (F re: Mark Frost)

Mosquitoes, 132:24
Jenny and Mr. Talliaferro were still dancing, as were Mrs. Wiseman and the **ghostly** poet. (F re: Mark Frost et al)

Mosquitoes, 234:30
Mark Frost had roused and with a **ghostly** epigram had taken himself off to bed. (F)

Mosquitoes, 329:22
The street light sprayed his tall **ghostly** figure with shadows of bitten late August leaves . . . (F re: Mark Frost)

Mosquitoes, 334:30
. . . Mark Frost plunged his long ungovernable legs across the soft slumbrous glare of polished asphalt and clawed his panting, **ghostly** body through the opened doors out of which the conductor leaned . . . (F)

Sartoris, 26:12
Then the hill-man bought it and cut some of the trees . . . and whitewashed the remaining trees and ran his barn-and hog-and chicken-lot fences between their **ghostly** trunks. (F)

Sartoris, 60:6
Occasionally young Bayard or John would open the door and peer into the solemn obscurity in which the shrouded furniture loomed with a sort of **ghostly** benignance, like albino mastodons. (F)

Sartoris, 281:33
. . . they set off among **ghostly** shocks of corn, where every day Bayard kicked up a covey of quail, toward the woods. (young Bayard, Narcissa, Isom, and Caspey)

Sartoris, 317:3
The clamor of the dogs swelled just beneath them and the **ghostly** shapes of them shifted in the faint glow . . . (young Bayard and the MacCallum family)

GHOST-RIDDEN

Sartoris, 301:19
This should be Horace's day, and her own too—a surcease from that **ghost-ridden** dream to which she clung, waking. (Narcissa)

GHOSTS

Mosquitoes, 47:19
. . . amid the rich overripe odors of the ends of the earth—coffee and resin and tow and fruit—he walked, surrounded by **ghosts,** passing on. (Gordon)

Mosquitoes, 52:29

The warehouse loomed over them, and they passed into it and amid the **ghosts** of the ends of the earth. (Fairchild and Semitic man)

Mosquitoes, 242:12

". . . hovering over this American scene into which he has been thrust, the **ghosts** of the Emersons and Lowells and other exemplifiers of Education with a capital E . . ." (Semitic man to Mrs. Wiseman re: Fairchild)

Mosquitoes, 243:6

"No one needs freedom . . . He need only . . . let himself forget all this fetish of culture and education which his upbringing and the **ghosts** of those whom circumstance permitted to reside longer at college than himself . . ." (Julius to Mark Frost et al)

Sartoris, 12:13

. . . riders rode with saber or musket at arm's length before them lest they be swept from saddle by invisible boughs, and continued until the forest thinned with dawn-**ghosts** . . . (F re: Aunt Jenny telling a story)

Sartoris, 89:33, 90:1

. . . chairs and sofas like patient **ghosts** holding lightly in dry and rigid embrace yet other **ghosts**—a fitting place for dead Sartorises to gather and speak among themselves of glamorous and of disastrous days. (F)

Sartoris, 107:20, 21

The yard was desolate with **ghosts; ghosts** of discouraged weeds, of food in the shape of empty tins, broken boxes and barrels . . . (F)

Sartoris, 126:28

. . . Bayard's voice went on . . . surmounting the odor of cheap food too quickly cooked and of sharp, split whisky with **ghosts** of a thing high-pitched as a hysteria, like a glare of fallen meteors on the dark retina of the world. (F re: young Bayard)

Sartoris, 223:7

His voice trailed away among ancient phantoms of the soul's and body's fortitudes, in those regions of glamorous and useless strivings where such **ghosts** reside. (F re: Falls)

Sartoris, 323:5

. . . homely shapes like sad **ghosts** in the chill corpse-light—the woodpile; a farming tool; a barrel beside the broken stoop at the kitchen door where he had stumbled, supperward. (F re: young Bayard)

Sartoris, 380:14

The music went on in the dusk softly; the dusk was peopled with **ghosts** of glamorous and old disastrous things. (F)

GLORY

Mosquitoes, 73:1
"Mud and **glory,** or a bit of ribbon on a clean tunic." (Major Ayers to Fairchild et al)

Mosquitoes, 82:17
Sunset was in his eyes: a **glory** he could not see; and her taut simple body . . . was an ecstasy in golden marble . . . (F re: Gordon and Patricia)

Mosquitoes, 166:11
The mist without thinning was filling with light: an imminence of dawn like a **glory,** a splendor of trumpets unheard. (F)

Mosquitoes, 215:22
. . . soon they had passed the bronze nave of the river into the lake beneath the rushing soundless wings of sunset and a dying **glory** of day under the cooling brass bowl of the sky. (F re: David, Patricia, and swampman)

Mosquitoes, 269:23
Once there was a king who possessed all things. All things were his: power, and **glory,** and wealth, and splendor and ease. (Gordon to Patricia—a quote of Cyrano)

GOD[1]

Soldiers' Pay, 45:10
In the next room Cadet Lowe waked from a chaotic dream, opening his eyes and staring with detachment, impersonal as **God,** at lights burning about him. (F)

Soldiers' Pay, 50:13
Listen, when I first saw you my love for you was like—my love was like—my love for you—**God,** if I only hadn't drunk so much last night I could say it my love for you my love is love is like . . . (Lowe re: Mrs. Powers)

Soldiers' Pay, 58:15
"It is more than that: it is by such as this that man may approach nearest to **God.**" . . . He stared unblinking into the sun-filled sky: drowned in his eyes was a despair long since grown cool and quiet. (rector to Jones)

Soldiers' Pay, 58:23
"Our **God,**" continued Jones, "need not be compassionate, he need not be very intelligent. But he must have dignity. (to rector)

1 See also Appendix A, p. 129.

Soldiers' Pay, 63:3

"If a man, if a single man, could be freed for a moment from the forces of gravity . . . what would he do? He would be a **god,** the lord of life . . ." (Jones to rector)

Soldiers' Pay, 65:25

And **God** only knew what this great lump of a divine meant by bread for the belly and no bread for the palate. (Jones re: rector)

Soldiers' Pay, 83:8

What luck that girl has in playing her parts. Even **God** helps her . . . You cat! she's pretty and you are jealous. (Mrs. Powers re: Cecily)

Soldiers' Pay, 89:10

His round face was enigmatic as a **god's,** his clear obscene eyes showed no emotion. (F re: Jones)

Soldiers' Pay, 112:11

Elms surrounded the courthouse and beneath the trees, on scarred and carved wood benches and chairs the city fathers, progenitors of solid laws and solid citizens who believed in Tom Watson and feared only **God** and drouth . . . (F)

Soldiers' Pay, 235:20

Solemnly the clock on the courthouse, staring its four bland faces across the town, like a kind and sleepless **god,** dropped eleven measured golden bells of sound. (F)

Soldiers' Pay, 288:4

"But then, I am not **God,** you know." (Jones to Joe Gilligan)

Soldiers' Pay, 313:7

He trod on with the moon in his face, seeing the cupolaed clock squatting like a benignant **god** on the courthouse against the sky, staring across the town with four faces. (F re: Joe Gilligan)

Soldiers' Pay, 317:8

"**God** bless you, Joe. Was it on my account you decided to stay?" (rector to Joe Gilligan)

Soldiers' Pay, 317:21

"I thought you'd a said **God,** reverend." (Joe Gilligan to rector)

Soldiers' Pay, 317:22, 22

"**God** is circumstance, Joe. **God** is in this life. We know nothing about the next. That will take care of itself in good time." (rector to Joe Gilligan)

Soldiers' Pay, 319:11

It was nothing, it was everything; then it swelled to an ecstasy, taking he white man's words as readily as it took his remote **God** and made a personal Father of Him. (F re: Negroes singing)

47

Mosquitoes, 36:32

"He is just the man to help you figure out some way to get **God** into the mercantile business." (Fairchild to Hooper et al)

Mosquitoes, 37:5

"Well, there's nothing better on **God's** green earth than Rotary." (Hooper to Talliaferro et al)

Mosquitoes, 40:17

"**God** must look about our American scene with a good deal of consternation, watching the antics of these volunteers who are trying to help Him." (Fairchild to Semitic man et al)

Mosquitoes, 40:23

"Other nations seem able to entertain the possibility that **God** may not be a Rotarian or an Elk or a Boy Scout after all." (Fairchild to Semitic man et al)

Mosquitoes, 47:3

fool fool you have work to do o cursed **god** cursed and forgotten... (Gordon)

Mosquitoes, 48:16

... strangle your heart with hair fool fool cursed and forgotten of **god** (Gordon)

Mosquitoes, 95:8

"Mark stop that thing as you love **God**." (Mrs. Wiseman to Mark Frost re: the victrola)

Mosquitoes, 97:27

"But I don't like to see a human being being arrogating to himself the privileges and pleasures of providence. Quelling nuisances is **God's** job. (Fairchild to Semitic man et al)

Mosquitoes, 125:21

... her spirit lay on its belly above Maggiore, watching little white boats no bigger than water beetles, and the lonely arrogant eagles aloft in blue sunshot space surrounded and enclosed by mountains cloud brooded, taller than **God**. (F re: Patricia)

Mosquitoes, 185:23

"Just think how much better Dawson would have done you than **God** did." (Mrs. Wiseman to Miss Jameson)

Mosquitoes, 210:1

"Why, only that tactless and well meaning **God** of yours alone knows." (Semitic man to Fairchild et al)

Mosquitoes, 229:24

"I don't mean exactly that they go to church when they are told to, for instance, because their elders expect it of them—though **God** only knows what other reason they could possibly have for going to church as it is conducted nowadays . . ." (Semitic man to Fairchild)

Mosquitoes, 321:8
"We don't like to see any one violate laws we observed, and get away with it. **God** knows, heaven is a dry reward for abnegation." (Semitic man to Fairchild)

Mosquitoes, 321:19
"But when some foreign matter like a leaf or a fold of drapery (kept there in defiance of gravity by **God** only knows what) draws the imagination . . ." (Fairchild to Semitic man)

Sartoris, 43:17
But now the railway belonged to a syndicate and there were more than two trains on it that ran from Lake Michigan to the Gulf of Mexico . . . while John Sartoris slept among the martial cherubim and the useless vainglory of whatever **God** he did not scorn to recognize. (F)

Sartoris, 87:23
"I'll be damned," he said, "if I haven't got the triflingest set of folks to make a living for **God** ever made." (old Bayard to Simon)

Sartoris, 296:20
From time to time Isom entered with hot bread, while Simon stood overlooking the field somewhat as Caesar must have stood looking down into Gaul, once it was well in hand, or the Lord **God** Himself when He contemplated His latest chemical experiment and saw that it was good. (F)

GOD'S WORK

Soldiers' Pay, 280:18
You say right off that this is **God's work.** But it must be a woman: no man could be so utilitarian. (F)

GODS

Soldiers' Pay, 63:4
"If a man . . . could be freed for a moment from the forces of gravity . . . He would be a god, the lord of life, causing the high **gods** to tremble on their thrones: he would thunder at the very gates of infinity like a mailed knight." (Jones to rector)

Soldiers' Pay, 137:22
"My dear ma'am, who am I to refuse what the **gods** send" (Jones to Cecily)

Soldiers' Pay, 151:11

. . . he should be a gladiator or a statesman or a victorious general: someone hard and ruthless would expect nothing from her, of whom she would expect nothing. Like two **gods** exchanging golden baubles. (Gilligan's reverie re: Mrs. Powers and a man)

Mosquitoes, 41:33

". . . I have no quarrel with education. I don't think it hurts you much, except to make you unhappy and unfit for work, for which man was cursed by the **gods** before they had learned about education." (Semitic man to Fairchild et al)

Mosquitoes, 153:12

"The humble laborer, Mr. Gordon: she too, has her place in the scheme of things; she, too, has given something to the world, has walked where **gods** have trod." (Mrs. Maurier)

Mosquitoes, 164:9

The first morning of Time might well be beyond this mist, and trumpets preliminary to a golden flourish; and held in suspension in it might be heard yet the voices of the Far **Gods** on the first morning saying, It is well: let there be light. (F)

Mosquitoes, 174:8

High cypress roots thrust up like weathered bones out of a green scum and a quaking neither earth nor water, and always those bearded eternal trees like **gods** regarding without alarm . . . (F re: David and Patricia)

Sartoris, 198:7

"You forget that lying is a struggle for survival," he said, "little puny man's way of dragging circumstances about to fit his preconception of himself as a figure in the world. Revenge on the sinister **gods**." (Horace to Narcissa)

Sartoris, 198:23

Above the arched canyon of the street the sinister **gods** stared down with pale unwinking eyes. (F)

GODSEND

Sartoris, 10:11

The war was a **godsend** to Jeb Stuart . . . (F re: Aunt Jenny's story)

GODSPEED

Mosquitoes, 326:17

"And her Lochinvar to wish her **godspeed,** watching her ankles as she got into the carriage." (Semitic man to Fairchild re: Mrs. Maurier)

GOLDEN RULE

Mosquitoes, 65:4

"I have a better idea than that, for both sexes: your photograph on one side and the **golden rule** on the other." (Mrs. Wiseman to Major Ayers et al re: a decanter for laxative salts)

GOSPEL

Soldiers' Pay, 261:17

Funny going's on in that house. And a preacher of the **gospel**, too. Even if he is Episcopal. (voices in the town re: the rector)

GRAIL-LIKE

Sartoris, 272:14

And he drew a long and affecting picture, of high, **grail-like** principles and of patient abnegation. (F re: Simon)

HALO

Soldiers' Pay, 94:17

The light passing through her fine hair gave her a **halo** and lent her frail dress a fainting nimbus about her crumpling body like a stricken poplar. (F re: Cecily)

Mosquitoes, 139:4

. . . her hair lent to Jenny's divine body a **halo** like an angel's. (F)

HALO MOTIF

Soldiers' Pay, 7:19

So he sat in a smoldering of disgusted sorrow, not even enjoying his Pullman perogatives, spinning on his thumb his hat with its accursed **white band.** (F re: Julian Lowe)

Soldiers' Pay, 7:23

"Ah, go to hell," he returned sourly and Yaphank doffed his tortured **hat.** (Lowe to Yaphank)

Soldiers' Pay, 221:16

Jones, watching the **light in her fine hair,** lazy and yellow as an idol, Jones released her at last. (Cecily)

Soldiers' Pay, 222:3

He considered moving beyond her so that she must face the light and leave his own face in the shadow . . . The **light in her hair,** caressing the shape of her cheek. (Jones and Cecily)

Soldiers' Pay, 222:28

Light in her hair was the thumbed **rim of a silver coin,** the divan embraced her quietly and light quietly followed the long slope of her limbs. (F re: Cecily)

Soldiers' Pay, 226:12

The divan embraced her in its impersonal clasp. **Light** like the thumbed **rim of a coin about her indistinct face** . . . (F re: Cecily)

Soldiers' Pay, 227:22

Light in her hair, her mouth speaking and the vague, crushed shape of her body. (F re: Cecily)

Soldiers' Pay, 228:29

Her body was a vague white shape as he entered the room again and **light** was the thumbed **rim of a coin about her head.** (F re: Cecily)

Mosquitoes, 83:15

Exemplum of Pete's straw hat used as an ironic halo. Pete loomed beyond her: the last **light** in the world was concentrated in the implacable **glaze of his hat,** leaving the atmosphere about them darker still . . . (F re: Pete and Jenny)

Mosquitoes

Pete's hat used as an ironic halo.
55:22,   55:23,   58:15,   59:21,   59:23,   83:15,   107:25,   133:12,
175:24,   253:7,   253:10,   253:12,   253:14,   253:15,   253:21,   253:25,
253:32,   254:1,   254:2,   254:8,   254:13,   254:16,   254:17,   254:18,
254:19,   274:15,   274:22,   274:23,   274:28,   277:1,   286:18,   287:13,
287:15,   288:8,   288:11,   294:9,   300:25,   301:24,   302:8

Sartoris, 148:21

A car approached and slowed to the curb and shut off engine and lights, and in the tiered windows **heads** leaned, **aureoled against the lighted rooms behind,** without individuality, feminine, distant, delicately and divinely young. (F)

Sartoris, 148:29

. . . the slender **heads** leaned **aureoled with bright hair in the lighted windows** and the soft clapping drifted after them for a long while, fainter and fainter in the silver silence and the moon's infinitude. (F)

HEAVEN

Soldiers' Pay, 71:18

"Yes, I stumbled over that pail of water the doctor keeps just inside the front door, doubtless for the purpose of making his parishioners be sure they really require help from **heaven** . . ." (Jones to Cecily)

Soldiers' Pay, 199:30

(If there's justice in **heaven,** I'll get him next time.) (girl dancing)

Soldiers' Pay, 317:29

"We make our own **heaven** or hell in this world." (rector to Joe Gilligan)

Soldiers' Pay, 317:32

"Who knows; perhaps when we die we may not be required to go anywhere nor do anything at all. That would be **heaven.**" (rector to Joe Gilligan)

Soldiers' Pay, 317:33

"Or other people make our **heaven** and hell for us." (Joe Gilligan to rector)

Mosquitoes, 32:9

His brothers were various and they attained their several milieus principally by chance; milieus ranging from an untimely **heaven** via some one else's horse and a rope and a Texas cottonwood . . . to a state legislature via some one else's votes. (F re: Talliaferro)

Mosquitoes, 52:14

"We've got to fix our idea on a terrestrial place. Though we know it's second rate, that's the best we can do. But your people have got all **heaven** for your old home town, you know." (Fairchild to Semitic man)

Mosquitoes, 186:31

The water was an unbearable glitter, the forest was a bronze wall cast at a fearful heat and not yet cooled, and no breeze was anywhere under the world's **heaven.** (F)

Mosquitoes, 228:30

"We were taught to believe that duty is infallible or it wouldn't be duty, and if it were just unpleasant enough, you got a mark in **heaven,** sure. . . ." (Fairchild to Semitic man)

Mosquitoes, 241:15

"Perhaps there is a **heaven,** after all." (Semitic man to Fairchild et al)

Sartoris, 42:12

"All folks talkin' 'bout **heaven** ain't gwine dar," . . . (Elnora singing)

Sartoris, 42:21

. . . the sound of the crickets and of the frogs upon the silver air mingled and blended inextricably with the dying fall of Elnora's voice: "All folks talkin' 'bout **heaven** ain't gwine dar."

Sartoris, 67:24

"I don't know where they'll be, but no Sartoris is going to stay in **heaven** any longer than he can help." (Miss Jenny to Narcissa)

Sartoris, 93:8

The unturned corners of man's destiny. Well, **heaven,** that crowded place, lay just beyond one of them, they claimed . . . (F)

Sartoris, 93:10

. . . **heaven** filled with every man's illusion of himself and with the conflicting illusions of him that parade through the minds of other illusions. (F)

Sartoris, 126:12

. . . a meteoric violence like that of fallen angels, beyond **heaven** or hell and partaking of both . . . (F re: young Bayard)

Sartoris, 150:15, 16

"Is dis **heaven**?" one murmured after a time.

"Dey wouldn't let you in **heaven**, wid likker on yo' breaf and no hat, feller," another said. (Negroes to one another)

Sartoris, 199:31

. . . she had as many sins as her ordinary behavior could take care of, particularly as she had old Bayard's soul to get into **heaven** somehow also, what with him and young Bayard tearing around the country every afternoon at the imminent risk of their necks. (F re: Miss Jenny)

Sartoris, 258:10

"Like I dreamed in a fevver from **heaven** to Hell. I know what you do I know more than you think I see men vist you with bitter twangs." (note to Narcissa)

Sartoris, 296:32

. . . Simon brought in . . . a cake baked cunningly with whisky and nuts and fruits and ravishing as odors of **heaven** and treacherous and fatal as sin . . . (F)

HEAVENLY

Soldiers' Pay, 319:24

There was no organ; no organ was needed as above the harmonic passion of bass and baritone soared a clear soprano of women's voices like a flight of gold and **heavenly** birds. (F re: Negroes singing)

Mosquitoes, 213:31

The man stood on the veranda and watched her while she poured dippersful of **heavenly** water on her head. (F re: the swampman and Patricia)

Mosquitoes, 255:19

Into Jenny's **heavenly** eyes there welled momentarily a selfless emotion, temporarily pure and clean. (F)

HEAVENS

Soldiers' Pay, 117:26

He entered the house again, and they crossed grass beneath the imminent **heavens**. (F re: rector, Mr. Saunders, and Mrs. Powers)

HEAVEN-TREES

Sartoris, 165:30
. . . a brick building from which there came a steady, unbroken humming and about which in the spring gnarled **heaven-trees** swung ragged lilac bloom against the harsh ocher and Indian red of a clay cut-bank. (F)

HEAV'N

Soldiers' Pay, 315:6
'Ah, Moon of my Delight, that knows't no wane, The Moon of **Heav'n** is rising once again: How oft hereafter rising shall she look Through this same Garden after me—in vain!' (Jones)

HELL[1]

Soldiers' Pay, 9:17
"Why, poor soldier," said his friend, tearfully, "all alone in no man's land and no matches. Ain't war **hell**? I ask you." (Yaphank to companion)

Soldiers' Pay, 10:26
"Listen, think of having to go to work again when you get home. Ain't war **hell**?" (Yaphank to Lowe)

Soldiers' Pay, 136:17
Or perhaps they were portraits of the Ancient Mariner at different ages before he wore out his albatross. (F)
(Not even a dead fish could make a man look like that, thought Jones . . . No wonder the parson believes in **hell**.)

Soldiers' Pay, 196:20
"Look at them, Joe," Mrs. Powers said, "sitting there like lost souls waiting to get into **hell**." (re: ex-soldiers at a dance)

Soldiers' Pay, 247:12, 13
It is **hell** without you I miss you and I love you like **hell**. (Lowe in letter to Mrs. Powers)

Soldiers' Pay, 278:22
But he had soldiered after a fashion and he liked and respected Dr. Mahon, refusing to believe that simply because Dr. Mahon was Episcopal he was going to **hell** as soon as he died. (F re: the Baptist minister)

Soldiers' Pay, 317:29
"Remember, I am an old man, Joe. Too old for bickering or bitterness. We make our own heaven or **hell** in this world." (rector to Joe Gilligan)

---

1 See also Appendix A, p. 129.

Soldiers' Pay, 317:33

"Or other people make our heaven and **hell** for us." (Joe Gilligan to rector)

Mosquitoes, 131:8

"Whatever you believe, you'll always annoy some one, but you yourself will follow and bleed and die for it in the face of the law, **hell** or high water." (Semitic man to Fairchild)

Sartoris, 126:13

... he fell to talking of the war. Not of combat, but ... of meteoric violence like that of fallen angels, beyond heaven or **hell** and partaking of both ... (young Bayard)

Sartoris, 258:10

"Like I dreamed in a fevver from heaven to **Hell**. I know what you do I know more than you think I see men vist you with bitter twangs." (in a note to Narcissa from an admirer)

Sartoris, 321:32

That would account for it ... that he too was dead and this was **hell**, through which he moved for ever and ever with an illusion of quickness, seeking his brother who in turn was somewhere seeking him, never the two to meet. (young Bayard)

HERESEY MOTIF

Soldiers' Pay, 288:23

"Napoleon thought that his actions were important, Swift thought his emotions were important, Savonarola thought his **beliefs** were important. And they were." (Jones to rector et al)

HERMIT-PRIEST

Soldiers' Pay, 265:8

If Cellini had been a **hermit-priest** he might have imagined her, Mrs. Powers thought, wishing mildly she could see the other naked. (re: Cecily)

HOLLY

Sartoris, 60:8

... already in their minds the room was associated with death, an idea which even the **holly** and tinsel of Christmastide could not completely obscure. (F re: young Bayard and John)

Sartoris, 61:6

... Jeb Stuart himself, perhaps, on his glittering garlanded bay or with his sunny hair falling upon fine broadcloth beneath the mistletoe and **holly** boughs of Baltimore in '58. (F)

Sartoris, 349:20

And after dark, somewhere a dance, with **holly** and mistletoe and paper streamers, and the girls he had always known . . . (young Bayard)

HORN MOTIF

Mosquitoes, 211:22

Evening came sad as **horns** among the trees . . . huge trees brooded bearded and ancient as prophets out of Genesis. (F re: the swamp)

HUMILITY

Mosquitoes, 41:2

"Do you think your new ideal of willynilly Service without request or recourse is better than your old ideal of **humility**?" (Semitic man to Talliaferro)

IMMACULATE

Soldiers' Pay, 45:2

Gilligan . . . slept beside her, his boots . . . innocent and awkward upon a white spread of rented cloth, **immaculate** and impersonal. (Joe Gilligan and Mrs. Powers)

Soldiers' Pay, 58:8

. . . from the Gothic mass of the church the spire rose, a prayer imperishable in bronze, **immaculate** in its illusion of slow ruin across motionless young clouds. (F)

Soldiers' Pay, 65:5

After the **immaculate** naked morning, the interior of the hall vortexed with red fire. (F)

Soldiers' Pay, 74:11

I'll see about you later, he promised her mentally sitting to **immaculate** linen. (Jones re: Emmy)

Soldiers' Pay, 129:16

. . . the rain had ceased and long lances of sunlight piercing the washed **immaculate** air struck sparks amid the dripping trees. (F)

Soldiers' Pay, 133:18

The sun broke suddenly through the rain and long lances of sunlight piercing the washed **immaculate** air struck sparks amid the dripping trees. (F)

Soldiers' Pay, 168:25

The rector sat at his desk, a pen poised above an **immaculate** sheet, but he was not writing. (F)

Soldiers' Pay, 204:18
The boy's ironed face was a fretted fatuity above his **immaculate** linen. (F re: Lee Rivers)

Soldiers' Pay, 209:18
Mr. Rivers' ironed face, above the **immaculate** linen, met her and she grasped his arm. (F re: Lee Rivers at the dance)

Soldiers' Pay, 257:20
"Well," she remarked with comfortable curiosity, peering into the white calm face of the tall dark woman in her dark dress with its **immaculate** cuffs and collar . . . (Mrs. Burney to Mrs. Powers)

Soldiers' Pay, 286:6
Soon the evening star would be there above the poplar tip, perplexing it, **immaculate** and ineffable, and the poplar was vain as a girl darkly in an arrested passionate ecstacy. (F)

Soldiers' Pay, 291:9
. . . the slow hands of dusk had removed him as cleanly as the prestidigitator rieves a rabbit from an **immaculate** hat. (F re: Jones)

Soldiers' Pay, 307:24
Her face pallid and calm beneath her small white and black hat, above her **immaculate** collar. (F re: Mrs. Mahon)

Mosquitoes, 14:10
He employed his **immaculate** linen handkerchief reluctantly before thrusting the bottle beneath his coat. (F re: Talliaferro)

Mosquitoes, 76:30
The captain was busy with a wisp of cotton waste, hovering about the engine, dabbing at its **immaculate** anatomy with needless maternal infatuation. (F)

Mosquitoes, 193:14
"Finish your drink. O **immaculate** cherubim," he said, going on down the passage. (Semitic man to Fairchild)

Mosquitoes, 273:14
. . . dusk came across the simple **immaculate** domes of the city and into the court, stilling the sound of birds so that the lilac silence of the court was teased only by the plashing of water . . . (F)

Sartoris, 94:18
The walls were an **immaculate** new gray, with a reproduction of a Corot and two spidery dry-points in narrow frames . . . (F re: Dr. Alford's office)

Sartoris, 108:21
Upon the wall above the paper-filled fireplace a framed lithograph of an Indian maiden in **immaculate** buckskin leaned her naked bosom

above a formal moonlit pool of Italian marble. (F re: Beard's home)

Sartoris, 170:28
The lower casements stood open on gently billowing curtains; on the sill you expected to see a scrubbed wooden bowl, or at least an **immaculate** and supercilious cat. (F re: home of Horace and Narcissa)

Sartoris, 218:30
Old man Falls . . . came into town through the yet horizontal sunlight of morning, and in his dusty, neat overalls he now sat opposite old Bayard in **immaculate** linen and a geranium like a merry wound. (F)

IMMACULATELY

Soldiers' Pay, 190:18
Boys of both sexes swayed arm in arm, taking sliding tripping steps waiting for the music and the agile youth, lounging **immaculately,** said: "Have this dance?" (ex-soldiers at dance)

Soldiers' Pay, 208:3
She stood up in the car, looking about. One lounging **immaculately,** smoking, strolled past. "Oh, Lee," she called, in happy relief, "here I am." (Cecily to Rivers)

Soldiers' Pay, 300:25
A dog saw it also and bayed: a mellow, long sound that slid **immaculately** down a hill of silence, yet at the same time seemed to linger about her like a rumor of a far despair. (Emmy viewing the moon)

Mosquitoes, 25:31
Mr. Talliaferro echoed her **immaculately,** taking to himself the showman's credit. (re: Mrs. Maurier)

IMMEMORIAL

Sartoris, 280:26
Sometimes they sang—quavering, wordless chords in which plaintive minors blent with mellow bass in **immemorial** and sad suspense, their grave dark faces bent to the flames and with no motion of lips. (F re: Negroes)

IMMINENCE

Mosquitoes, 127:12
Mr. Talliaferro envied that chair with a surge of fire like an adolescent's in his dry bones . . . that surge of **imminence** and fire and desolation . . . leaving a thin salty taste on his tongue. (F)

Mosquitoes, 166:10
The mist without thinning was filling with light: an **imminence** of dawn like a glory, a splendor of trumpets unheard. (F)

IMMORTAL

Mosquitoes, 11:6
What this room troubled was something eternal in the race, something **immortal**. (F)

Sartoris, 126:14
. . . a meteoric violence like that of fallen angels, beyond heaven or hell and partaking of both: doomed immortality and **immortal** doom. (F re: young Bayard)

IMMORTALITY

Mosquitoes, 184:7
"Dawson clings to his conviction for the old reason, it's good enough to live with and comfortable to die with—like a belief in **immortality**." (Mrs. Wiseman to Semitic man et al)

Sartoris, 126:13
. . . beyond heaven or hell and partaking of both: doomed **immortality** and immortal doom. (F re: young Bayard)

IMMORTALS

Mosquitoes, 52:32
"Well, I'm like the rest of you **immortals**: I've got to pass the time in some way in order to gain some idea of how to pass eternity," the Semitic man answered. (to Fairchild)

INCANTATION

Soldiers' Pay, 309:16
The small stream murmured busily like a faint **incantation** and repeated alder shoots leaned over it Narcissus-like. (F)

INFINITUDE

Sartoris, 45:9
From her silver casement the moon looked down upon the valley dissolving in opaline tranquillity into the serene mysterious **infinitude** of the hills . . . (F)

Sartoris, 148:32
. . . the soft clapping drifted after them for a long while, fainter and fainter in the silver silence and the moon's **infinitude**. (F)

INFINITY

Soldiers' Pay, 63:5
"He would be a god . . . he would thunder at the very gates of infinity like a mailed knight." (Jones to rector)

Sartoris, 375:19
. . . the blue changeless hills beyond, and beyond that, the ramparts of infinity itself. (F)

INTOLERANCE

Mosquitoes, 116:4
"There were a bunch of brokendown preachers: head full of dogma and intolerance and a belly full of big meaningless words." (Fairchild to Josh)

INVIOLATE

Sartoris, 301:13
Yet that brought back the original distaste and dread: the possibility that the intactness of her deep and heretofore inviolate serenity might be the sport of circumstance . . . (Narcissa)

INVOCATION

Soldiers' Pay, 158:5
At the foot of the hill a dogwood tree spread flat palm-like branches in invocation among dense green, like a white nun. (F)

ISRAELITES

Mosquitoes, 251:9
"Interesting, anyway," the Semitic man said, "to reduce the spiritual progress of the race to terms of an emotional migration; esthetic Israelites crossing unwetted a pink sea of dullness and security." (to Mrs. Wiseman et al)

JESUS

Soldiers' Pay, 170:23
"Bless de Lawd, done sont you back ter yo' mammy. Yes, Jesus! Ev'y day I prayed and de Lawd heard me." (Callie to Donald Mahon)

Soldiers' Pay, 296:5
"Well, Jesus! we all gwine dat way, some day. All roads leads to de graveyard." (Negro to Loosh)

Soldiers' Pay, 313:13
". . . sweet chariot, comin' fer to ca'y me home . . . yes Jesus, comin' fer to ca'y me hoooooome . . ." (Negroes singing)

Soldiers' Pay, 319:13, 15
Feed Thy Sheep, O **Jesus.** All the longing of mankind for a Oneness with Something, somewhere. Feed Thy Sheep, O **Jesus** . . . (Negroes singing)

Soldiers' Pay, 319:21
Feed Thy Sheep, O **Jesus.** The voices rose full and soft. (Negroes singing)

Mosquitoes, 40:30
The Semitic man said: "My people produced **Jesus,** your people Christianized him. And ever since you have been trying to get him out of your church." (to Talliaferro et al)

JEW

Mosquitoes, 42:19
"For some reason one can be a Catholic or a **Jew** and be religious at home. But a Protestant at home is only a Protestant." (Semitic man to Fairchild et al)

Mosquitoes, 193:1
It was Fairchild and the fat **Jew,** but they passed his door and entered the room next to his, from which he heard . . . sounds of activity that culminated in a thin concussion of glass and glass. (Pete listening)

Mosquitoes, 193:5
"My God, man"—the fat **Jew's** voice—"what have you done? Do you really think we can move this boat?" (Semitic man to Fairchild)

JOHN

Sartoris, passim
John Sartoris, Colonel

Sartoris, passim
John Sartoris, Lieutenant, grandson of old Bayard and brother of young Bayard

JOSEPH (JOE)

Soldiers' Pay, passim
Joseph (**Joe,** Yaphank) Gilligan, veteran of W.W.I.
Reverend **Joe** Mahon, rector of the Episcopal church

Mosquitoes, passim
Joe Ginotta, brother of Pete

JOSHUA (JOSH)

Mosquitoes, passim
Josh (Gus, Theodore) Robyn, brother of Patricia and nephew of Mrs. Maurier

JUDGEMENT

Sartoris, 74:22
"It was a **judgement** on 'em, taking John instead of that other one."
(Aunt Sally to Narcissa)

Sartoris, 89:2
"He ought to have a wife," . . . "Let him get a son, then he can break his neck as soon and as often as he pleases. Providence doesn't seem to have any **judgement** at all," . . . (Miss Jenny to old Bayard re: young Bayard)

Sartoris, 115:31
At the door and with one foot raised to the running-board, he made a final stand against the subtle powers of evil **judgement.** (F re: Simon pausing before getting into the car)

KINGDOM OF GOD

Soldiers' Pay, 317:24
"God is in this life. We know nothing about the next. That will take care of itself in good time. 'The **Kingdom of God** is in man's own heart,' the Book says." (rector to Gilligan)

KNEEL

Mosquitoes, 26:33
". . . how was it those old people used to put it, about pausing on Life's busy highroad to **kneel** for a moment at the Master's feet? . . ." (Mrs. Maurier to Talliaferro)

KNELT

Soldiers' Pay, 170:26
She **knelt** beside Donald's chair, putting her hands on his face. (Callie)

Mosquitoes, 179:7
David **knelt** beside her and spoke her name again, and she sat up. (re: Patricia)

Mosquitoes, 190:32
"Do something quick, David," she told him, staring at him, and he lowered her awkwardly and **knelt** beside her, supporting her head. (re: Patricia)

Sartoris, 117:13
But Simon **knelt** in the floor with his eyes shut tightly and the air-blast toying with the grizzled remnant of his hair, holding the switch with both hands. (F)

Sartoris, 215:3

But immediately he recovered himself and turned his head and lifted the garment and laid his face against it, defiantly and deliberately, and **knelt** so for a time. (young Bayard)

LAWD

Soldiers' Pay, 170:23

"Yes, Jesus! Ev'y day I prayed, and de **Lawd** heard me." (Callie to Donald Mahon)

Soldiers' Pay, 171:18

"**Lawd**! ter hear de day when white man tell me Mist' Donald don't wanter see me!" (Callie to Joe Gilligan)

Sartoris, 24:11, 11

Sinner riz fum de moaner's bench,
Sinner jump to de penance bench;
When de preacher ax 'im whut de reason why,
Say, "Preacher got de woman jes' de same ez I."
　　　Oh **Lawd**, oh, **Lawd**!
Dat's whut de matter wid de church today. (Elnore)

Sartoris, 66:22

"Lemme tell you somethin', nigger," Simon said. "De good **Lawd** done took keer of you fer a long time, now, but He ain't gwine bother wid you always." (to Caspey)

Sartoris, 83:9

"And you better thank de good **Lawd** fer makin' yo' haid ez hit is. You go'n git dat mare, and save dat nigger freedom talk fer town-folks: dey mought stomach it." (Simon to Caspey)

Sartoris, 113:8

"Hit's de **Lawd's** blessin' you and her ain't bofe gone in it, like you is whenever Mist' Bayard'll let you." (Elnore to Isom)

Sartoris, 117:18, 19

"Dat's de way you stops it, **Lawd**! Dat's de way you stops it, **Lawd**!" Simon chanted, keeping the switch covered with his hands while Bayard hammered at them with his fist. (Simon to young Bayard re: car)

Sartoris, 149:22

"Oh, **Lawd**," the negro wailed. "Mr. Bayard!" The air-blast stripped his words away like leaves. "Lemme out, Mr. Bayard!" (re: car)

Sartoris, 150:18

"Ef de **Lawd** don't take no better keer of me dan He done of dat hat, I don't wanter go dar, noways," . . . (one Negro to another re: heaven)

Sartoris, 212:20

"Whut in de **Lawd**'s name," Simon said, "is you been into now?" (to young Bayard)

Sartoris, 274:31

"Thank de **Lawd**, we got dat offen our mind," Simon said, and he came and lowered himself to the top step, groaning pleasurably. (to old Bayard)

Sartoris, 275:22

"**Lawd**, Cunnel, I ain't got no fawty cents, en you knows it. Can't dey do widout dat, after gittin' de balance of it?" (Simon to old Bayard)

LIGHT (OF CREATION)

Mosquitoes, 164:10

The first morning of Time might well be beyond this mist, and trumpets preliminary to a golden flourish; and held in suspension in it might be heard yet the voices of the Far Gods on the first morning saying, It is well: let there be **light**. (F)

LITANY

Soldiers' Pay, 219:22

. . . young Robert repeated tirelessly: "What did you do in the war? Did you kill folks?" . . . young Robert, refraining his **litany**, caught Jones' yellow, fathomless eye, like a snake's, and young Robert's spine knew an abrupt, faint chill. (Robert Saunders to Jones)

LORD

Soldiers' Pay, 63:3

"He would be a god, the **lord** of life, causing the high gods to tremble on their thrones . . ." (Jones to rector re: man)

Soldiers' Pay, 111:15, 17

(S'what I say: if the **Lord** had intended folks to fly around in the air He'd 'a' give 'em wings.)
(Well, he's been closter to the **Lord**'n you'll ever git.) (townspeople)

Soldiers' Pay, 152:21

The rector wrote "The **Lord** is my shepherd: I shall not want."

Soldiers' Pay, 297:20

(I am the Resurrection and the Life, saith the **Lord** . . .) (F)

Mosquitoes, 35:17

"I am glad to see how you boys are carrying on the good work; I might say, the Master's work, for it is only by taking the **Lord** into our daily lives—" (Hooper to Talliaferro et al)

Mosquitoes, 151:6

. . . they lay with their backs to each other . . . "Three years . . . Good **Lord**." (Jenny to Patricia re: a club)

Mosquitoes, 193:13

"Good **Lord**," the other man said again. "Finish your drink. O immaculate cherubim," . . . (Semitic man to Fairchild)

Sartoris, 25:18

. . . for Simon had sisters in the **Lord** in this kitchen, and presently he let himself into the yard and followed the gravel driveway around to the back. (F)

Sartoris, 30:27

"Thank you. Well, thank the **Lord**, that's over," she added. "It's too bad folks haven't the sense or courage to send out invitations, then shut up the house and go away." (Miss Jenny to Narcissa)

Sartoris, 37:34

"Thank the **Lord** he hasn't thought about bringing his horse in with him." (Miss Jenny to Simon re: old Bayard)

Sartoris, 67:21

". . . I believe these Sartorises and all their possessions just set out to plague and worry me. Thank the **Lord**, I won't have to associate with 'em after I'm dead." (Miss Jenny to Narcissa)

Sartoris, 70:11

"And let me know what you hear from Horace. Thank the **Lord**, it's just a glass-blowing machine and not a war widow." (Miss Jenny to Narcissa)

Sartoris, 151:14

"My mother saw to it that I drank a good cup of bark tea when I come sulking to the table and wouldn't eat," Aunt Sally stated, "but folks nowadays think the good **Lord**'s going to keep 'em well and them lifting no finger. (to Narcissa)

Sartoris, 153:2

"I thank the **Lord** sometimes you and Horace ain't any blood of mine, the way you all go on." (Aunt Sally to Narcissa)

Sartoris, 200:16

"And then there'll be hell to pay. **Lord** knows what it'll be—maybe he and Isom will take his car and that tractor and hold a steeple-chase with 'em." (Miss Jenny to Narcissa)

Sartoris, 296:20

From time to time Isom entered with hot bread, while Simon stood overlooking the field somewhat as . . . the **Lord** God Himself when He contemplated his latest chemical experiment . . . (F)

Sartoris, 379:23

"I reckon the **Lord** knows His business, but I declare, sometimes . . . Play something." (Miss Jenny to Narcissa)

MADONNA AND CHILD

Mosquitoes, 17:21, 23

She extended to him a dull lead plaque from which in dim bas-relief of faded red and blue simpered a **Madonna** with an expression of infantile astonishment identical with that of Mrs. Maurier, and a **Child** somehow smug and complacent looking as an old man. (F re: Mrs. Maurier and Talliaferro)

MAJESTIC

Sartoris, 35:5

. . . Bayard now sat here . . . transferring bourbon whisky from a small rotund keg to a silver-stoppered decanter, while two dogs watched him with **majestic** gravity. (F)

MAJESTICAL

Sartoris, 4:6

With his race's fine feeling for potential theatrics he drew himself up and arranged the limp folds of the duster . . . into Simon's wizened black face there came an expression indescribably **majestical** as he touched his whiphand to his hat-brim. (F)

MAJESTICALLY

Sartoris, 272:25

. . . a small, reluctant ebon negro in somber, overlarge black—where the parson **majestically** made room for him, contriving by some means to focus attention on him. (F)

MAJESTY

Mosquitoes, 8:11

They came cityward lustful as country boys, as passionately integral as a college football squad; pervading and monstrous but without **majesty**: a biblical plague seen through the wrong end of a binocular . . . (F)

Mosquitoes, 8:13

. . . the **majesty** of Fate become contemptuous through ubiquity and sheer repetition. (F)

Sartoris, 24:19

But the house had burned, and some of the trees had been felled to make room for an architectural garbling so imposingly terrific as to possess a kind of **majesty**. (F)

MARK

Mosquitoes, passim
Mark Frost, poet, guest on Mrs. Maurier's yacht

MASTER (DIVINITY)

Mosquitoes, 26:33
". . . Mr. Talliaferro, how was it those old people used to put it, about pausing on Life's busy highroad to kneel for a moment at the **Master's** feet?" (Mrs. Maurier to Talliaferro et al)

Mosquitoes, 35:16
"I am glad to see how you boys are carrying on the good work; I might say, the **Master**'s work, for it is only by taking the Lord into our daily lives—" (Hooper to Talliaferro et al)

Sartoris, 104:15
"I am the first of my name to see sixty years that I know of. I reckon Old **Marster** is keeping me for a reliable witness to the extinction of it." (old Bayard to Dr. Peabody)

Sartoris, 113:3
"Pappy out dar talkin' to Ole **Marster** agin," Isom told her. (to his mother)

METHODIST

Sartoris, 9:28
. . . once he hunted a pack of fox hounds through a rustic tabernacle in which a **Methodist** revival was being held . . . (F re: Bayard Sartoris of Carolina)

MINISTER

Soldiers' Pay, 187:21
Mrs. Worthington ate too much and suffered from gout and a flouted will. So her church connection was rather trying to the **minister** and his flock. (F)

Soldiers' Pay, 278:16
The Baptist **minister,** a young dervish in a white lawn tie, being most available, came and did his duty and went away. (F re: minister that married Donald Mahon and Mrs. Powers)

Soldiers' Pay, 295:10
(. . . a Boy Scout bugler furnished by the young Baptist **minister,** a fiery-eyed dervish, who had served in the Y.M.C.A.) (F)

Soldiers' Pay, 307:3
"Joe, come with me."
"To a **minister**?" he asked with resurgent hope.

"No, just as we are. Then when we get fed up all we need do is wish each other luck and go our ways." (Mrs. Mahon and Joe Gilligan)

Sartoris, 274:23
He faced Simon again. "Deacon Strother," he said "ez awdained **minister** of de late Fust Baptis' Church . . ." (parson to committee)

Sartoris, 274:24
"Deacon Strother," he said, "ez . . . recalled **minister** of de pupposed Secon' Baptis' Church, en chairman of dis committee . . ." (parson to committee)

MIRACULOUS

Soldiers' Pay, 289:18
"You had expected great things from marriage, hadn't you? Sort of a **miraculous** rejuvenation?" (Jones to Mrs. Mahon)

MIRACULOUSLY

Soldiers' Pay, 292:14
"Did you—?" the question hung poised in the dusk between them and here was the evening star bloomed **miraculously** at the poplar's tip and the slender tree was a leafed and passionate Atalanta, poising her golden apple. (Joe Gilligan and Mrs. Mahon)

MISTLETOE

Sartoris, 61:6
. . . Jeb Stuart . . . on his glittering garlanded bay or with his sunny hair falling upon fine broadcloth beneath the **mistletoe** and holly boughs of Baltimore in '58. (F)

Sartoris, 349:20
And after dark, somewhere a dance, with holly and **mistletoe** and paper streamers, and the girls he had always known . . . (young Bayard)

MONASTIC MOTIF

Mosquitoes, 335:2
Three gray, softfooted priests had passed on, but in an interval hushed by **windowless old walls** there lingers yet a thin celibate despair. (F)

Mosquitoes, 337:9
Above the **hushing walls,** a thing wild and passionate, remote and sad; shrill as pipes, and yet unheard. (F)

Mosquitoes, 340:13
The priests cross themselves while the nuns of silence blend anew

their breath, and pass on: soon the high **windowless walls** have hushed away their thin celibate despair. (F)

MONK

Sartoris, 364:5

Above them stood a waiter with a head like a **monk's** and as Bayard passed he saw that the diamond was missing from Harry's tie, and he heard their bitter suppressed voices as their hands struggled over something on the table . . . (young Bayard re: Harry Mitchell and a woman)

MORAL COURAGE

Soldiers' Pay, 237:9

He walked on trying to bolster his **moral courage**, trying not to look like a sneaking nigger, but, in spite of him, it seemed that every dark quiet house stared at him . . . (George Farr)

MORTALITY

Sartoris, 375:5

. . . an orotund solemnity having no more to do with **mortality** than the bindings of books have to do with their characters . . . (F re: Miss Jenny at the cemetery)

NAVE

Soldiers' Pay, 160:2

The sun was yet in the tops of the trees and here were cedars unsunned and solemn, a green quiet **nave**. (F)

Mosquitoes, 83:1

You might, by listening, have heard a slow requiem in this tall **nave**, might have heard here the chanted orisons of the dark heart of the world turning toward slumber. (F)

Mosquitoes, 215:21

. . . soon they had passed from the bronze **nave** of the river . . . the rushing soundless wings of sunset and a dying glory of day under the cooling brass bowl of the sky. (David, Patricia, and swampman)

NEMESIS

Soldiers' Pay, 217:2

The man was a **nemesis**; every time she had seen him since that first day at luncheon with Uncle Joe, he had flouted her, had injured her with diabolic ingenuity. (Jones and Cecily)

NEW TESTAMENT

Sartoris, 214:19

The book was a **New Testament;** on the flyleaf in faded brown, "To my son, John, on his seventh birthday, March 16, 1900, from his Mother." He had one exactly like it . . . (young Bayard)

Sartoris, 215:4

Then he rose and gathered up the **book** and the trophy and the coat and crossed to his chest of drawers and took from it a photograph. (young Bayard)

Sartoris, 215:22

Soon a blaze, pale in the sunny air, and when the wood was burning strongly he laid the coat and the **Testament** and the trophy and the photograph on the flames . . . (young Bayard)

NIMBUS

Soldiers' Pay, 94:18

The light passing through her fine hair gave her a halo and lent her frail dress a fainting **nimbus** about her crumpling body like a stricken poplar. (F re: Cecily)

Soldiers' Pay, 214:7

He saw her as she entered the door and, rising, he saw her pause on seeing him . . . with light toying with her white dress, giving it a shallow **nimbus,** she came tap-tapping on her high heels toward him. (George Farr and Cecily)

Soldiers' Pay, 221:24

He could see a **nimbus** of light in her hair and the shape of her, but her face he could not see. (Jones and Cecily)

Soldiers' Pay, 319:19

Worn-out red-gutted fields were now alternate splashes of soft black and silver; trees had each a silver **nimbus,** save those moonward from them, which were sharp as bronze. (F)

NIMBUSED

Soldiers' Pay, 224:26

Her unseen face **nimbused** with light and her body, which was no body, crumpling a dress that had been dreamed. (F re: Cecily)

Mosquitoes, 49:8

Looking through the tall pickets into Jackson square was like looking into an aquarium . . . in the center of it Andrew's baroque plunging stasis **nimbused** about with thin gleams as though he too were recently wetted. (F re: Gordon)

NUN

Soldiers' Pay, 158:6

At the foot of the hill a dogwood tree spread flat palm-like branches in invocation among dense green, like a white **nun.** (F)

NUNS

Soldiers' Pay, 61:13

Against a privet hedge would soon be lilies like **nuns** in a cloister and blue hyacinths swung soundless bells, dreaming of Lesbos. (F)

Mosquitoes, 337:9

The priests draw nearer, touching one another, leaning diffidently above the beggar in the empty street while silence comes slow as a procession of **nuns** with breathing blent. (F)

Mosquitoes, 340:12

The priests cross themselves while the **nuns** of silence blend anew their breath, and pass on: soon the high windowless walls have hushed away their thin celibate despair. (F)

OLD TESTAMENT

Soldiers' Pay, 66:31

There were books everywhere—on shelves, on window ledges, on the floor: Jones saw the **Old Testament** in Greek in several volumes . . . (F)

OMNIPOTENCE

Soldiers' Pay, 63:8

"As it is, he must ever have behind his mind a dull wonder how anything composed of fire and air and water and **omnipotence** in equal parts can be so damn hard." (Jones to rector re: man)

Soldiers' Pay, 271:30

She looked at Emmy impersonal as **Omnipotence,** helping Donald with effacing skill, seeming to envelop him, yet never touching him. (Mrs. Powers)

Sartoris, 179:14

. . . a darkly gallant shape romantic with smuggled edibles, with strong, hard hands that smelled always of a certain thrilling carbolic soap—a being something like **Omnipotence** but without awesomeness . . . (Narcissa re: Horace)

ONENESS

Soldiers' Pay, 319:14

Feed Thy Sheep, O Jesus. All the longing of mankind for a **Oneness** with Something, somewhere. (F)

ORISONS

Soldiers' Pay, 123:21

Steam rose again about Emmy's forearms . . . glass gleamed under Mrs. Powers' toweling and a dull parade of silver took the light mutely, hushing it as like two priestesses they repeated the **Orisons** of Clothes. (F)

Mosquitoes, 83:2

You might . . . have heard a slow requiem in this tall nave, might have heard here the chanted **orisons** of the dark heart of the world turning toward slumber. (F)

PADRE

Soldiers' Pay, 104:21

"Let's go to the garden so I can have a cigarette." (Mrs. Powers) "You could have it here. The **padre** wouldn't mind, I bet." (Joe Gilligan)

Soldiers' Pay, 189:18

A large new flag is flown and the enemy fires at it vainly with .22 rifles. The men on our side cheer, led by the **padre**. (F re: soldiers)

Soldiers' Pay, 303:31

"The **padre**'s lucky though." . . . "Well, if you have hard luck and your hard luck passes away, ain't you lucky?" (Joe Gilligan to Mrs. Mahon)

Soldiers' Pay, 316:16

"It wasn't no fight; he was too busy getting away. It takes two folks to fight, **padre**." (Joe Gilligan)

Soldiers' Pay, 317:4

"Well, **padre**, to tell the truth, I ain't got any. If it's the same to you I think I'll stay on with you a while longer." (Joe Gilligan re: his plans)

PANDEMONIUM

Mosquitoes, 297:17

The very waiters themselves he did not know . . . and the noise was now a turgid **pandemonium** of saxophones and drums and, riding above it like distracted birds, a shrill and metallic laughter of women ceaseless and without joy . . . (Pete at the restaurant)

Sartoris, 133:8

Bayard crouched on its shoulders and dragged its mad head around and they swept down the lane, spreading **pandemonium** among the horses and mules tethered and patient about the blacksmith shop . . . (young Bayard)

Sartoris, 306:34

The din of them swelled to a shrill **pandemonium** and the pack boiled into the road in a chaos of spotted hides and flapping tongues and ears. (F re: the dogs)

Sartoris, 359:30

The shabby man was talking . . . his voice hoarse and importunate against the meaningless **pandemonium** of horns and drums. (F)

PANES (STAINED GLASS)

Sartoris, 8:27

On either side of this door was a narrow window set with leaded **panes of varicolored glass** that, with the bearer of them, constituted John Sartoris' mother's deathbed legacy to him, which his youngest sister had brought from Carolina in a straw-filled hamper in '69. (F re: Miss Jenny)

Sartoris, 9:5

This was Virginia DuPre . . . bringing with her the clothing in which she stood and a wicker hamper filled with **colored glass.** (F)

Sartoris, 19:11

But the door was closed now, and what light passed through the **colored panes** was richly solemn. (F)

Sartoris, 297:5

The sun lay hazily in the glowing west, falling levelly through the the windows . . . dreaming in mellow gleams among its placid rotundities and on the **colored panes** in the fanlight high in the western wall. (F)

PARABOLIC

Soldiers' Pay, 247:15

Birds across the lawn **parabolic** from tree to tree mocked him . . . and a tree near the corner of the veranda, turning upward its cease- less white-bellied leaves, was a swirling silver veil stood on end . . . (F re: Jones)

Soldiers' Pay, 252:6

Birds in a wind across the lawn, **parabolic** from tree to tree, and a tree at the corner of the house turning upward its white-bellied leaves in a passionate arrested rush . . . (F)

PARADISE

Mosquitoes, 272:21

I desire a thing that . . . dead remembering it I would cling to this world though it be as a beggar in a tattered robe; yea, rather that would I than a king among kings amid the soft and scented sounds of **paradise.** (Gordon)

PARADISE LOST

Soldiers' Pay, 136:20
Jones rose and from a bookcase he got a copy of **"Paradise Lost"** (cheerful thing to face a sinner with, he thought), and returned to his chair. (F)

Mosquitoes, 116:7
". . . one instructor always insisted that the head devil in **Paradise Lost** was an inspired prophetic portrait of Darwin . . ." (Fairchild to Josh)

PARISHIONER

Soldiers' Pay, 58:10, 14
"My one sincere **parishioner,**" murmured the divine. . . .
"**Parishioner,** did I say? It is more than that: it is by such as this that man may approach nearest to God." (rector to Jones)

PARISHIONERS

Soldiers' Pay, 71:18
"Yes, I stumbled over that pail of water the doctor keeps just inside the front door, doubtless for the purpose of making his **parishioners** be sure they really require help from heaven, on their second visit," . . . (Jones to Cecily)

Soldiers' Pay, 104:23
"I am considering his **parishioners.** What would they think to see a dark strange woman smoking a cigarette on the rectory porch at eight o'clock in the morning?" (Mrs. Powers to Joe Gilligan)

PARSON

Soldiers' Pay, 90:23
"The others? They went to the station, the railroad station. You know: where the trains come in. The **parson's** son or something is coming home this afternoon." (Jones to Cecily)

Soldiers' Pay, 98:1
"So he come home. Well, well. I'm glad on the **parson's** account. Pretty decent feller." (Mr. Saunders to his wife re: Donald Mahon)

Soldiers' Pay, 136:17
(Not even a dead fish could make a man look like that, thought Jones, refusing the dyspeptic gambit of their fretful painted eyes. No wonder the **parson** believes in hell.) (Jones re: portrait in rector's room)

Soldiers' Pay, 257:13
And here approaching was that strange woman staying at **Parson**

Mahon's, the one that come here with him and that other man, getting herself talked about, and right. (Mrs. Burney re: Mrs. Powers)

Soldiers' Pay, 280:25, 26

. . . after a while those who had said I told you so when Miss Cecily Saunders let it be known that she would marry the **parson**'s son and who said I told you so when she did not marry the **parson**'s son forgot about it. (F)

Soldiers' Pay, 317:26

"God is circumstance, Joe. God is in this life. We know nothing about the next. . . ."

"Ain't that a kind of funny doctrine for a **parson** to get off?" (rector and Joe Gilligan)

Mosquitoes, 221:30

"And, of course, when they got back home they wouldn't tell, not until another **parson** turned up and everything was all regular again." (Fairchild to Semitic man re: women)

Sartoris, 272:25

Brother Moore created a mild disturbance in the rear of the group, emerging presently by the agency of sundry willing hands . . . where the **parson** majestically made room for him, contriving by some means to focus attention on him. (F)

Sartoris, 273:6, 8

. . . then he and the **parson** held a brief whispered conversation. He opened the notebook and fumbled at the leaves . . . until the **parson** leaned over his shoulder and found the proper page . . . (Brother Moore)

Sartoris, 273:14

"Brudder Mo' will now read out de amount," the **parson** intoned.

Sartoris, 273:20

"Louder," the **parson** rumbled, with just a trace of impatience. (to Brother Moore)

Sartoris, 273:29

The deputation milled again, and Brother Moore faded briskly into the rear of it. The **parson,** however, still retained his former attitude of fateful and impressive profundity. (F)

Sartoris, 274:11

Old Bayard tramped in the hall again and emerged, flapping a check in his hand. "Here." he commanded, and the **parson** approached the railing and took it . . . (F)

Sartoris, 274:21

The deputation had already stirred with a concerted movement, but the **parson** halted them with a commanding hand. (F)

Sartoris, 275:10
At last the **parson** spoke. "You fergot de fawty cents, white folks."
(to old Bayard)

Sartoris, 276:3
"Give 'em that money!" old Bayard thundered. "I reckon you can
pay forty cents of it, at least." Simon rose reluctantly, and the
parson approached. (to Simon)

PARSONS' HOMES

Mosquitoes, 219:11
"I thought Gretna Green was a place where they used to go to get
marriage licenses in a hurry," . . . (Fairchild)
"It was, once," Mayor Ayers agreed. "But during the Great Fire
all the registrars' and **parsons' homes** were destroyed."

PASSION WEEK

Mosquitoes, 339:23
"That's what it is. Genius." . . . "It is that **Passion Week** of the
heart, that instant of timeless beatitude which some never know,
which some, I suppose, gain at will, which others gain through an
outside agency like alcohol . . ." (Gordon to Fairchild)

PATRIARCHAL MOTIF

Mosquitoes, 171:4
The mist broke raggedly and drifted in sluggish wraiths that seemed
to devour all sound, swaying and swinging like huge spectral apes
from tree to tree, rising and falling, revealing sombre **patriarchs** of
trees hiding them again. (F re: David and Patricia in the swamp)

Mosquitoes, 174:15
It was she who found the fallen tree, who first essayed its oozy
treacherous bark and first stood in the empty road stretching monotonously in either direction between battalioned **patriarchs** of trees.
(F re: Patricia)

Mosquitoes, 213:15
Then the sound came again across the afternoon, among the **patriarchal** trees—a faint fretful sound. (F re: David and Patricia in the
swamp)

PEACE

Soldiers' Pay, 12:31
"My God," repeated the conductor. "If we ever have another **peace**
I don't know what the railroads will do. I thought war was bad, but
my God." (to Lowe and Yaphank)

Soldiers' Pay, 21:2
"But say, these men are dangerous. What are you good for, if you can't preserve the **peace**?" (soldier to policeman)

Soldiers' Pay, 28:3
Gilligan raised his glass, squinting at it. "Here's to **peace**," he said. "The first hundred years is the hardest." (to Lowe)

Soldiers' Pay, 135:26
"Has the army disbanded already? . . . We had scarcely enough men to fight a war with, but with a long **peace** ahead of us—man, we are helpless." (Jones to Joe Gilligan)

Soldiers' Pay, 174:31
. . . they sat thinking of home . . . of **peace** and quiet and all homely things, of a time when there was no war. (F re: Captain Green and Sergeant Madden)

Soldiers' Pay, 176:20
Outside, Madden felt mud, knew darkness and damp, he smelled food and excrement and slumber beneath a sky too remote to distinguish between **peace** and war. (F)

Soldiers' Pay, 297:10
Rest in **Peace** in cast repetition: Our motto is one for every cemetery, a cemetery for everyone throughout the land. (F)

Soldiers' Pay, 301:22
She felt freer, more at **peace** with herself than she had felt for months. (Mrs. Mahon)

Mosquitoes, 73:9
"But even **peace** can't last forever, can it?" the Semitic man added. "It'll last a while—this one. Can't have another war right off." (Major Ayers)

Mosquitoes, 210:24
"For heaven's sake." the other exclaimed, "let us have this one drink in **peace**." (Semitic man to Fairchild)

Sartoris, 15:33
The glade lay quiet and empty of threat beneath the mounting golden day; laked in it lay a deep and abiding **peace** like golden wine . . . (F)

Sartoris, 64:31
"De folks wuz white American soldiers and dey egvised us to pick out a hole and stay dar fer a while, ef us wanted de **peace** and comfort of de war." (Caspey to Simon)

Sartoris, 169:3
These homes were quite old, in appearance at least, and set well back from the street and its dust, they emanated a gracious and

benigh **peace**, steadfast as a windless afternoon in a world without motion or sound. (F)

Sartoris, 169:8
"Perhaps this is the reason for wars," he said. "The meaning of **peace**." (Horace to Narcissa)

Sartoris, 175:25
He was a lawyer . . . he contemplated returning to his musty office with a glow of . . . not eagerness, no: of deep and abiding unreluctance, almost of pleasure. The meaning of **peace**. Old unchanging days; unwinged perhaps, but disastrous, too. (Horace)

Sartoris, 176:7
"The meaning of **peace**," he said to himself once more, releasing the grave words one by one within the cool bell of silence into which he had come . . . again, hearing them linger with a dying fall pure as silver and crystal struck lightly together. (Horace)

Sartoris, 182:18
. . . in his moments of rhapsody over the realization of the meaning of **peace** and the unblemished attainment of it, as "Thou still unravished bride of quietness." (F re: Horace)

Sartoris, 229:28
Finally old Bayard tramped from the house and mounted his horse and rode away, leaving Miss Jenny to wear her rage out upon the empty air, and then there was **peace** for a time. (F)

Sartoris, 245:9
. . . the leaves hung motionless beneath the intermittent fingers of the sun, and she sat also without life . . . thinking that there would be **peace** for her only in a world where there were no men at all. (Narcissa)

Sartoris, 254:8
Far above him now the peak among the black and savage stars, and about him the valleys of tranquillity and of **peace**. (young Bayard)

Sartoris, 254:22
The sun was gone, and twilight, foster dam of quietude and **peace**, filled the fading room, the evening had found itself. (F)

Sartoris, 352:28
". . . so many who burrow along like moles in the dark, or like owls, to whom a candle-flame is a surfeit. But not to those who carry **peace** along with them as the candle-flame carries light." (Horace writing a letter to Narcissa)

Sartoris, 380:35
Beyond Miss Jenny's trim, fading head the maroon curtains hung motionless; beyond the window the evening was a windless lilac

dream, foster dam of quietude and **peace**. (F — this is the last sentence in the book)

PEACEFUL

Soldiers' Pay, 237:31
Nothing save the **peaceful**, unemphatic sounds of night. (F re: George Farr)

Mosquitoes, 207:17
The Semitic man looked at him, then he too looked about the others and upon the now **peaceful** scene of their recent activities. (re: Talliaferro et al)

Sartoris, 2:25
After a while John Sartoris departed also, withdrawn rather to that place where the **peaceful** dead contemplate their glamorous frustrations . . . (F re: old Bayard thinking)

Sartoris, 4:21
. . . his employer had settled back for the changing and **peaceful** monotony of the four-mile drive. (Simon and old Bayard)

Sartoris, 13:18
. . . erratic bursts of musketry surged and trickled along the scattered outposts . . . the name Stuart speeding from picket to picket had peopled the blossoming **peaceful** woods with gray phantoms. (F)

Sartoris, 35:21
. . . the man on his horse and the ticked setter gravely beside him, while the descending evening of their lives drew toward its **peaceful** close upon the kind land that had bred them both. (F re: old Bayard)

Sartoris, 119:16
Town among its trees, its shady streets like green tunnels, along which tight lives accomplished their **peaceful** tragedies. (F)

Sartoris, 154:34
. . . she went to the window and stood there, between the parted curtains, looking out upon the black-and-silver world and the **peaceful** night. (Narcissa)

Sartoris, 180:7, 7
But now he lay in the adjoining room, voyaging in safe and glittering regions beyond the moon, and she lay in her dark bed, quiet, **peaceful**, a little too **peaceful** to sleep. (Horace and Narcissa)

Sartoris, 347:10
Bayard . . . was lost in a timeless region where he lingered unawake and into which he realized after a long while something was trying

to penetrate; watched its vain attempts with **peaceful** detachment. (young Bayard)

Sartoris, 371:29
. . . all the **peaceful** scents of summer came up on the sunny breeze, and sounds—birds, somewhere a Sabbath bell . . . (F)

Sartoris, 373:17
They entered the white folks' section and passed now between marble shapes bearing names . . . and dates in stark and **peaceful** simplicity in the impervious stone. (Miss Jenny and Isom in the cemetery)

Sartoris, 376:20
. . . she remembered something Narcissa had said once, about a world without men, and wondered if therein lay **peaceful** avenues and dwellings thatched with quiet . . . (Miss Jenny)

PEACEFULLY

Soldiers' Pay, 19:21
New York in a rosy glow of alcohol and sunset streamed past breaking into Buffalo, and with fervent new fire in them they remarked the station. Poor Hank now slept **peacefully** . . . (Lowe and Yaphank on the train)

Sartoris, 12:18
. . . they galloped again and crashed through astonished picket parties returning **peacefully** to camp. . . . (Aunt Jenny's story)

Sartoris, 101:21
. . . a room resembling a miniature cyclonic devastation mellowed **peacefully** over with dust ancient and undisturbed. (F re: Dr. Peabody's office)

Sartoris, 117:3
The wagon was moving drowsily and **peacefully** along the road. (F)

Sartoris, 137:4
. . . the handles of a plow stood at a gaunt angle while its share rusted **peacefully** in the undergrowth, the other implements rusted half concealed there—skeletons of labor healed over by the earth they were to have violated, kinder than they. (F)

Sartoris, 193:20
. . . they went on through the house, where all noises were remote and the furniture gleamed **peacefully** indistinct in the dying evening light. (Horace and Belle)

Sartoris, 218:26
At times she would cease and look at him and find that he was **peacefully** sleeping. (Narcissa and young Bayard)

Sartoris, 297:11

. . . November . . . when like a shawled matron among her children, the year dies **peacefully,** without pain and of no disease. (F)

Sartoris, 321:13

Buddy breathed on in the darkness, steadily and **peacefully.** (F)

Sartoris, 371:29

The curtains stirred **peacefully** at the windows, and all the peaceful scents of summer came up on the sunny breeze . . . (F)

Sartoris, 373:5

Simon's burying society had taken care of him, and after three weeks the mound was still heaped with floral designs from which the blooms had fallen, leaving a rank, lean mass of stems and **peacefully** rusting wire skeletons. (F)

PEACETIME

Soldiers' Pay, 98:28

"Well, an engagement in war time and an engagement in **peace time** are two different things." (Mrs. Saunders to her husband re: Cecily and Donald Mahon)

Mosquitoes, 73:7

"Staff tabs worth two on the breast: only see the breast from one side. Ribbon's good in **peacetime,** however." (Major Ayers to Semitic man et al)

Sartoris, 44:29

"Takes damn near as big a fool to get hurt in a war as it does in **peacetime.**" (young Bayard to old Bayard)

PENANCE

Sartoris, 24:8

Sinner riz fum de moaner's bench,
Sinner jump to de **pennance** bench; . . . (Elnore)

PETER (PETE)

Mosquitoes, passim

Pete Ginotta, an unexpected guest on the Nausikaa

PLOWMAN

Sartoris, 6:15

. . . presently they drove upon Bayard's own land and from time to time a **plowman** lifted his hand to the passing carriage. (Simon and old Bayard)

PRAY

Mosquitoes, 255:29

"Only he'd better show up soon . . . We've got to get back home."
(Patricia re: Gordon)

"Have you?" her aunt said with heavy astonished irony, "How are
you goinng, **pray?**" (Mrs. Maurier)

Sartoris, 153:12

"She ain't wiped off a picture frame in six months, to my certain
knowledge. And I've done everything but beg and **pray.**" (Aunt
Sally to Narcissa re: servant)

Sartoris, 236:16

" 'Madam,' he says, 'I was fo'ced to muss up yo' guest-room right
considerable. **Pray** accept my apologies, and have yo' nigger clean
it up and send the bill to me.' " (Falls telling a story to old Bayard)

PRAYED

Soldiers' Pay, 170:23

"Bless de Lawd, done sont you back ter yo' mammy. Yes, Jesus!
Ev'y day I **prayed,** and de Lawd heard me." (Callie to Donald
Mahon)

PRAYER

Soldiers' Pay, 58:7

. . . from the Gothic mass of the church the spire rose, a **prayer** imperishable in bronze, immaculate in its illusion of slow ruin across
motionless young clouds. (F)

PREACHER

Soldiers' Pay, 43:12

"We got to get him home first," Gilligan said. "I'll wire his folks
to-morrow—his old man is a **preacher,** see." (to Mrs. Powers re:
Donald Mahon)

Soldiers' Pay, 261:16

Funny goings-on in that house. And a **preacher** of the gospel, too.
Even if he is Episcopal. (voices in the town re: Reverend Mahon)

Sartoris, 24:9, 10

. . . When de preacher ax 'im whut the reason, why,
   Say, "**Preacher** got de women jes' de same ez I." (Elnore)

Sartoris, 324:13

His spent blood, wearied with struggling, moved through his body
in slow beats, like the rain, wearing his flesh away. It comes to all
. . . Bible . . . some **preacher,** anyway. Maybe he knew. Sleep. It
comes to all. (young Bayard)

PREACHERS

Soldiers' Pay, 290:18

"For the good of your soul," Gilligan told him joyously. "You might say that's what running with **preachers** does for you . . .?" (to Jones)

Mosquitoes, 115:21

"It was a kind of funny college I went to. A denominational college, you know, where they turned out **preachers**." (Fairchild to Josh)

Mosquitoes, 116:3

"But I kind of got interested in learning things: I learned in spite of the instructors we had. They were a bunch of brokendown **preachers**: head full of dogma and intolerance and a belly full of big meaningless words." (Fairchild to Josh)

PRESBYTERIAN

Soldiers' Pay, 307:6

"Then when we get fed up all we need do is wish each other luck and go our ways." He stared at her, shocked. "Damn your **Presbyterian** soul, Joe. Now you think I'm a bad woman." (Mrs. Mahon to Gilligan)

PRIEST

Soldiers' Pay, 265:8

If Cellini had been a hermit-**priest** he might have imagined her, Mrs. Powers thought . . . (re: Cecily)

Soldiers' Pay, 281:7

Miss Cecily Saunders was safely married—though nobody knows where they was from the time they drove out of town in George Farr's car until they was properly married by a **priest** in Atlanta the next day . . . (F)

Soldiers' Pay, 288:27

"Very apt, Mr. Jones," murmured Mrs. Mahon above the suggested triangle of her cuffs and collar. "A soldier, a **priest** and a dyspeptic."

Mosquitoes, 92:4

"You simply cannot tell what they're going to do," she said . . . seeing again Major Ayers' vanishing awkward shape and Fairchild leaning over the rail and howling after him like a bullvoiced Druid **priest** at a sacrifice. (Mrs. Maurier to Mrs. Wiseman et al)

Mosquitoes, 337:31

The beggar makes no reply, he does not stir; and the second **priest** leans nearer his pale half-shadowed face. (F)

Mosquitoes, 338:2

The third **priest** leans down, raising his voice. Brother (F)

Mosquitoes, 338:10

The beggar does not move and the **priest's** voice is a dark bird seeking its way from out a cage. (F)

Mosquitoes, 339:12

At last one **priest,** becoming bolder, leans yet nearer and slips his hand beneath the beggar's sorry robe, against his heart. It is cold. (F)

PRIESTESSES

Soldiers' Pay, 123:20

Steam rose again about Emmy's forearms, wreathing her head . . . glass gleamed under Mrs. Powers' toweling and a dull parade of silver took the light mutely, hushing it as like two **priestesses** they repeated the orisons of Clothes. (F)

PRIESTS

Mosquitoes, 335:1

Three gray, softfooted **priests** had passed on, but in an interval hushed by windowless old walls there lingers yet a thin celibate despair. (F)

Mosquitoes, 335:13

The three **priests** pass on: the walls have hushed their gray and unshod feet. (F)

Mosquitoes, 336:32

Three more **priests,** barefoot, in robes the color of silence, appear from nowhere. They are speeding after the first three, when they spy the beggar beneath the stone gate. (F)

Mosquitoes, 337:6

The **priests** draw nearer, touching one another, leaning diffidently above the beggar in the empty street while silence comes slow as a procession of nuns . . . (F)

Mosquitoes, 337:25

The beggar yet sleeps, shaping his stolen crust, and one of the **priests** says, Do you require aught of man, Brother? (F)

Mosquitoes, 338:2

Beneath his high white brow he is not asleep, for his eyes stare quietly past the three **priests** without remarking them. (F)

Mosquitoes, 338:13

The three **priests** gaze at one another. The beggar lies motionless beneath the stone gate. (F)

Mosquitoes, 340:11

The **priests** cross themselves while the nuns of silence blend anew their breath, and pass on: soon the high windowless walls have hushed away their thin celibate despair. (F)

PROCESSION (FUNERAL)

Soldiers' Pay, 295:23

(The **procession** moved slowly across the square. Country people, in town to trade, turned to stare vacuously . . . the city fathers . . . having reached the point where death would look after them instead of they after death, waked and looked and slept again. . . .) (F re: Donald Mahon's funeral)

Soldiers' Pay, 297:9

(The **procession** moved beneath arching iron letters. Rest in Peace in cast repetition: Our motto is one for every cemetery, a cemetery for everyone throughout the land . . .) (F re: Donald Mahon's funeral)

PROCESSIONAL

Soldiers' Pay, 281:24

. . . tall jade candlesticks of leaves beneath the blue cathedral of sky across which, in hushed **processional,** went clouds like choirboys slow and surpliced. (F)

PROFANE

Sartoris, 105:2

Then the sound of their voices moved on down the corridor toward the stairs, and still quarreling loudly and, on old Bayard's part, with **profane** emphasis, the voices died away. (F)

Sartoris, 172:31

Flem himself was presently manager of the city light and water plant . . . three years ago, to old Bayard's **profane** astonishment and unconcealed annoyance, he became vice president of the Sartoris bank . . . (F)

Sartoris, 251:27

It was a brutal tale, without beginning, and crassly and uselessly violent and at times **profane** and gross, though its very wildness robbed it of offensiveness, just as its grossness kept it from obsenity. (F re: young Bayard's story of his brother, John)

PROFANELY

Sartoris, 135:3

. . . Dr. Peabody **profanely** bandaged Bayard's head and gave him a drink from the bottle which resided in the cluttered wastebasket . . . (young Bayard)

Sartoris, 140:31

They drank again, and Hub began to borrow cigarettes of Bayard and he too became a little **profanely** and robustly anecdotal in his country idiom, about whiskey and girls and dice . . . (young Bayard)

Sartoris, 238:28

Between the two of them they got old Bayard on the early train, still protesting **profanely,** like a stubborn and bewildered ox. (Miss Jenny and Dr. Alford)

PROFANITY

Sartoris, 250:30

His breath hissed between his teeth and he screamed, a wordless sound that merged into a rush of **profanity** . . . he watched her with wide intent eyes in which terror lurked, and mad, cold fury and despair. (young Bayard and Narcissa)

Sartoris, 373:15

Isom dropped obediently to the ground and the birds threatened him with a final burst of . . . **profanity.** (F)

PROPHETIC

Mosquitoes, 116:8

". . . one instructor always insited that the head devil in *Paradise Lost* was an inspired **prophetic** portrait of Darwin . . ." (Fairchild to Josh)

PROPHETS

Mosquitoes, 211:26

. . . against the hidden flame of the west huge trees brooded bearded and ancient as **prophets** out of Genesis. (F)

PROTESTANT

Mosquitoes, 42:4

"But to go back to religion"—"the spirit **protestant** eternal," murmured the blond young man hoarsely—"do you mean any particular religion, or just the general teaching of Christ?" (to Fairchild et al)

Mosquitoes, 42:15

"Yes," Fairchild admitted. "I always think of the **Protestant** religion." (to Semitic man et al)

Mosquitoes, 42:19, 20

"For some reason one can be a Catholic or a Jew and be religious at home. But a **Protestant** at home is only a **Protestant**." (Semitic man to Fairchild et al)

Mosquitoes, 42:20

"It seems to me that the **Protestant** faith was invented for the sole purpose of filling our jails and morgues and houses of detention." (Semitic man to Fairchild et al)

Mosquitoes, 42:24

"How do young **Protestant** boys in small towns spend Sunday after-noons, with baseball and all such natural muscular vents denied them? They kill, they slay and steal and burn." (Semitic man to Fairchild et al)

PROVERBS

Mosquitoes, 37:24

"Our forefathers reduced the process of gaining money to **proverbs.** But we have beaten them; we have reduced the whole of existence to fetiches." (Fairchild to Semitic man)

PROVIDENCE

Soldiers' Pay, 63:20

"Anarchism? Surely. The hand of **Providence** with money-changing blisters. That is anarchism." (Jones to rector)

Soldiers' Pay, 63:22

"At least you admit the hand of **Providence.**" (rector to Jones)

Soldiers' Pay, 63:29

"How do you find the hand of **Providence** here?" he puffed around his pipe stem. (Jones to rector)

Soldiers' Pay, 155:9

"So you are meddling with **Providence,** are you?" "Wouldn't you have done the same?" she defended herself. (Dr. Baird and Mrs. Powers)

Mosquitoes, 97:26

"But I don't like to see a human being arrogating to himself the priv-ileges and pleasures of **providence.** Quelling nuisances is God's job." (Fairchild to Semitic man et al)

Mosquitoes, 97:28

"How about the instruments of **providence?**" (Semitic man)
"Oh, take another drink," Fairchild told him.

Mosquitoes, 131:11

"And those who die for causes will perish for any cause, the more tawdy it is, the quicker they flock to it. And be quite happy at it, too. It's a provision of **providence** to keep their time occupied." (Semitic man to Fairchild)

Mosquitoes, 328:1

"Perhaps it's a scheme of nature to provide for our Italian immi-grants. Or of **Providence.** Prohibition for the Latin, politics for the Irish, invented He them." (Semitic man to Fairchild et al)

Mosquitoes, 328:8

Fairchild continued: "Italians and Irish. Where do we homegrown Nordics come in? What has He invented for us?"

"Nothing," the Semitic man answered. You invented **Providence.**"

Sartoris, 9:32

In a spirit of fun, purely: he believed too firmly in **Providence,** as all his actions clearly showed, to have any religious convictions whatever. (F re: Bayard Sartoris of Carolina)

Sartoris, 74:18

"Even Lucy Cranston, come of as good people as there are in the state, acting like it was divine **providence** that let her marry one Sartoris and be the mother of two more. Pride, false pride." (Aunt Sally to Narcissa)

Sartoris, 89:1

"He ought to have a wife," . . . "Let him get a son, then he can break his neck as soon and as often as he pleases. **Providence** doesn't seem to have any judgement at all," . . . (Miss Jenny to old Bayard re: young Bayard)

PURGED

Soldiers' Pay, 129:9

"You poor child," Mrs. Powers said. She raised Emmy's face: it was calm, **purged.** She no longer felt superior to the girl. (F)

Soldiers' Pay, 225:9

Not an ivory carving: this would have body, rigidity; not an animal that eats and digests—this is the heart's desire **purged** of flesh. (Jones re: Cecily)

Sartoris, 171:33

"And the things themselves. Sheerly and tragically beautiful. Like preserved flowers, you know. Macabre and inviolate; **purged** and purified as bronze, yet fragile as soap bubbles." (Horace to Narcissa re: products of his glass-blowing)

PURGING

Sartoris, 9:17

. . . the history of the race had been raised from out the old miasmic swamps of spiritual sloth by two angels valiantly fallen and strayed, altering the course of human events and **purging** the souls of men. (F re: Aunt Jenny's story)

PURIFICATION

Sartoris, 73:21

. . . his grandson sat in his shredded clothes, and on his scratched face that look of one who has gained for an instant a desire so fine that its escape was a **purification,** not a loss. (F re: John Sartoris after a parachute jump)

PURIFIED

Sartoris, 171:33
"Like preserved flowers, you know. Macabre and inviolate; purged and **purified** as bronze, yet fragile as soap bubbles." (Horace to Narcissa)

PURITANS

Mosquitoes, 321:6
"If a man has had to deny himself any pleasures during his pleasuring years, he always likes to believe it was necessary. That's where you get your **Puritans** from." (Semitic man to Fairchild)

RACHEL

Sartoris, passim
Sis' **Rachel,** servant in the Mitchell home

RAPHAEL

Sartoris, passim
Raphael "Rafe" MacCallum, son of Virginus MacCallum

RECTOR

Soldiers' Pay, passim
Reverend Joe Mahon, **rector** of the Episcopal Church

RECTORY

Soldiers' Pay, 57:11
Sparrows were delirious in ivy and the rambling facade of the **rectory** was a dream in jonquils and clipped sward. (F)

Soldiers' Pay, 100:21
He picked up the object he had dropped in falling and crossed the **rectory** lawn through dew, toward the house. (Robert Saunders, Jr.)

Soldiers' Pay, 104:25
"I am considering his parishioners. What would they think to see a dark strange woman smoking a cigarette on the **rectory** porch at eight o'clock in the morning?" (Mrs. Powers to Joe Gilligan)

Soldiers' Pay, 114:30
They passed beneath the church spire and crossed the lawn. Mounting the steps of the rectory, they saw Mrs. Powers sitting with a book. (rector and Mr. Saunders)

Soldiers' Pay, 180:29

The rambling facade of the **rectory** dreamed in the afternoon above a lawn broken by geranium beds and a group of chairs beneath a tree. (F)

Soldiers' Pay, 284:7

He dreamed of her at night, he mistook other women for her, other voices for hers; he hung skulking about the **rectory** at all hours . . . (Jones re: Emmy)

Soldiers' Pay, 287:5

The canvas sagged under him and he rose and spun his chair so as to face the dreaming facade of the **rectory**. (Jones)

Soldiers' Pay, 313:17

In the garden the mocking bird that lived in the magnolia rippled the silence, and along the moony wall of the **rectory** from ledge to ledge, something crawled shapelessly. (F re: Gilligan observing Jones)

REJUVENATION

Soldiers' Pay, 289:19

"You had expected great things from marriage, hadn't you? Sort of a miraculous **rejuvenation**?" (Jones to Mrs. Mahon)

RELIGION

Mosquitoes, 41:11

"Are you opposed to **religion**, then—in its general sense, I mean?" (Fairchild to Semitic man et al)

Mosquitoes, 41:14, 16

"The only sense in which **religion** is general is when it benefits the greatest number in the same way. And the universal benefit of **religion** is that it gets the children out of the house on Sunday morning." (Semitic man to Fairchild et al)

Mosquitoes, 42:4, 6

"But to go back to **religion**"—"the spirit protestant eternal," murmured the blond young man hoarsely—"do you mean any particular **religion**, or just the teaching of Christ?" (to Fairchild et al)

Mosquitoes, 42:14, 16

"But when you say **religion**, you have a particular sect in mind, haven't you?" (Semitic man)

"Yes," Fairchild admitted. "I always think of the Protestant **religion**."

RELIGIO-SENTIMENTAL

Soldiers' Pay, 225:22

. . . Jones a fat Mirandola in a chaste nympholepsy, a **religio-senti-**

mental orgy in gray tweed shaping an insincere, fleeting articulation of damp clay to an old imperishable desire, building himself a papier mache Virgin ... (F)

RELIGIOUS
Mosquitoes, 42:19
"For some reason one can be a Catholic or a Jew and be **religious** at home. But a Protestant at home is only a Protestant." (Semitic man to Fairchild et al)

Sartoris, 9:33
... he believed too firmly in Providence, as all his actions clearly showed, to have any **religious convictions** whatever. (F re: Bayard Sartoris of Carolina)

RELIGIOUS SONG

Soldiers' Pay, 286:11
Half of the moon was a coin broken palely near the zenith and at the end of the lawn the first fireflies were like lazily blown sparks from cool fires. A negro woman passing crooned a **religious song**, mellow and passionless and sad. (F)

RELIGIOUS ZEAL

Soldiers' Pay, 57:6
"But one of my cloth is prone to allow his own soul to atrophy in his **zeal** for the welfare of other souls that—" (rector to Jones)

REQUIEM

Mosquitoes, 83:1
You might, by listening, have heard a slow **requiem** in this tall nave, might have heard here the chanted orisons of the dark heart of the world turning toward slumber. (F)

REST IN PEACE

Soldiers' Pay, 297:9
(The procession moved beneath arching iron letters. **Rest in Peace** in cast repetition: Our motto is one for every cemetery, a cemetery for everyone through the land ...) (F)

RESURRECTION

Soldiers' Pay, 297:20
(I am the **Resurrection** and the Life, saith the Lord. ...) ... (Whosoever believeth in Me, though he were dead. ...) ... (... yet shall he live. And whosoever liveth and believeth in Me shall never die. ...) (F)

Mosquitoes, 267:24

"It looks like it's up to us. Gordon ought to celebrate his **resurrection,** anyway." (Semitic man to Fairchild re: Gordon's return to the boat)

RETRIBUTION

Soldiers' Pay, 120:20

. . . her father desisted from the bottle long enough to woo and wed an angular shrew who, serving as an instrument of **retribution,** beat him soundly with stove wood in her lighter moments. (F re: Emmy's father)

REVEREND

Soldiers' Pay, 60:15

"The coins might be reduced again to bullion and coined over, and—" the **reverend** man looked at Jones in ecstasy—"the housewives could use the objects for fuel with which to cook food." (rector to Jones)

Soldiers' Pay, 79:23

Emmy vanished and he put his hands on the girl's shoulders. "Now what will you do? Call the **reverend?**" (Jones to Cecily)

Soldiers' Pay, 156:17

"Yes, **Reverend,** you let Mrs. Powers here advise you about that. I have every confidence in her judgement." (Dr. Baird to rector)

Soldiers' Pay, 316:23

"You damn right he did, **reverend.** I bet he was a son-of-a-gun in his day." (Gilligan to rector re: Donald)

Soldiers' Pay, 317:21

"Circumstance moves in marvelous ways, Joe." (rector)
"I thought you'd a said God, **reverend.**" (Gilligan)

Sartoris, 273:11

"How much is it, **reverend?**" old Bayard asked impatiently.
"Brudder Mo' will now read out de amount," the parson intoned.

REVIVAL

Sartoris, 9:28

. . . once he hunted a pack of fox hounds through a rustic tabernacle in which a Methodist **revival** was being held; and thirty minutes later . . . he returned alone and rode his horse into the ensuing indignation meeting. (F re: Bayard Sartoris of Carolina)

REV'UN

Soldiers' Pay, 107:28

"Mr. Gillmum, **Rev'un** say fer you to come to de house." (Othello)

RITUAL

Soldiers' Pay, 68:14

He placed the things upon the desk, before the propped photograph like a **ritual,** and propping his face in his earthy hands he took his ruined dream of his son into himself as one inhales tobacco smoke. (rector)

Soldiers' Pay, 198:13

She saw two heads as one head, cheek to cheek, expressionless and fixed as a **ritual** above a synchronization of limbs. (Mrs. Powers observing Cecily and Dr. Gary at the dance)

Mosquitoes, 117:15, 17

"It's young people who put life into **ritual** by making conventions a living part of life: only old people destroy life by making it a **ritual.** (Fairchild to Josh)

Mosquitoes, 208:18

. . . they found seats while Fairchild again assumed the **ritual** of his hidden suitcase. (Major Ayers et al)

Sartoris, 60:18

And after they went to England in '16 it was opened twice a year to be cleaned after the ancient **ritual** that even Simon had inherited from his forefathers . . . (F re: a room in the Sartoris home)

Sartoris, 140:22

Miss Jenny made a little wine of it every year. . . . Elder-flower wine. Like a **ritual** for a children's game; a game played by little girls in small pale dresses, between supper and twilight. (F)

Sartoris, 222:6

The parcel lay on his knees and he now opened it after the ancient laborious **ritual,** picking patiently at the pink knot . . . (old man Falls)

Sartoris, 234:31

"He has to kind of put a aidge on hisself, like he'd hold his ax to the grindstone," he said, squatting before the pungent curling of the smoke as though in a pagan **ritual** in miniature. (old man Falls to old Bayard)

RITUALISTIC

Sartoris, 59:28

. . . a place for his wife and his son John's wife and Miss Jenny to clean thoroughly twice a year and in which preceded by a **ritualistic** unswaddling of brown holland, they entertained their more formal callers. (F re: a room in the Sartoris home)

94

Sartoris, 281:27

. . . old Bayard would unlock his desk and fetch the silver-stoppered decanter and compound three toddies with **ritualistic** care. (F)

RITUALS

Soldiers' Pay, 282:5

He conducted services in . . . the church . . . while pigeons held their own crooning **rituals** of audible slumber in the spire that, arcing across motionless young clouds, seemed slow and imminent with ruin. (F re: rector)

ROBES (CHRISTENING)

Sartoris, 371:26

Narcissa and the nurse . . . had brought the baby, bathed and garnished and scented in his **ceremonial robes**, in to her . . . (young Bayard's son brought to Miss Jenny)

ROBES (CLERICAL)

Mosquitoes, 336:32

Three more priests, barefoot, in **robes** the color of silence, appear from nowhere. (F)

SABBATH

Sartoris, 276:15

In her room . . . she could still hear them—old Bayard's stormy rage and Simon's bland and plausible evasion, rising and falling on the drowsy **Sabbath** air. (Miss Jenny)

Sartoris, 348:34

Again a heavy explosion in the dusk ahead, and they debouched on to the square with its **Sabbath** calm, littered too with shattered scraps of paper. (F re: young Bayard and a Negro)

Sartoris, 371:31

. . . all the peaceful scents of summer came up on the sunny breeze, and sounds—birds, somewhere a **Sabbath** bell, and Elnora's voice . . . rich and mellow as she went about getting dinner. (F)

SAINT SULPICE

Sartoris, 61:22

Then the draft got him and bore him to France and the **Saint Sulpice** docks as one of a labor battalion, where he did what work corporals and sergeants managed to slough on his unmilitary shoulders . . . (F re: Caspey)

SALVATION

Soldiers' Pay, 57:8
"—that not only do not deserve **salvation,** but that do not particularly desire it," finished Jones. (to rector re: souls)

Soldiers' Pay, 58:22
"We purchase our **salvation** as we do our real estate. Our God," continued Jones, "need not be compassionate, he need not be very intelligent. But he must have dignity." (to rector)

Sartoris, 199:27
Miss Jenny said she was too far along to jeopardize **salvation** by driving to church at fifty miles an hour; that she had as many sins as her ordinary behavior could take care of ... (F)

SANCTIMONIOUS

Mosquitoes, 115:25
"He was a **sanctimonious** old fellow with a beard like a goat, and every year he offered a half scholarship to be competed for by young men working for him." (Fairchild to Josh re: a college trustee)

SANCTION

Mosquitoes, 324:28
"I imagine he—her father—was pretty near the end of his rope. Some government appointment, I imagine, brought him south: hijacking privileges with official **sanction,** you know." (Semitic man to Fairchild et al re: Mrs. Maurier's father)

SANCTIONED

Sartoris, 169:17
The cedars had been set out by an English architect of the '40's, who had built the house . . . in the funereal light Tudor which the young Victoria had **sanctioned** . . . (F)

SANCTIONING

Sartoris, 100:23
"I must protest against this," Dr. Alford said. "Mrs. Du Pre, I protest against a member of my profession **sanctioning,** even negatively, such a procedure." (re: old Bayard's wart)

SANCTUARY

Sartoris, 12:25
The others pursued the fleeing breakfasters for a short distance into the **sanctuary** of the woods, but most of them rushed on to the General's private commissary tent and emerged presently from the

cyclonic demolition of it, bearing plunder. (F re: Aunt Jenny's story)

SANTA CLAUS

Sartoris, 345:18
"Show de white folks yo' **Sandy Claus**." she prompted. (Negro mother to her children)

Sartoris, 345:22
"Show 'im," she repeated. "You want folks to think **Sandy Claus** don't know whar you lives at?" (Negro mother to her children)

SATAN MOTIF

Sartoris, 126:11, 12
... he fell to talking of the war. Not of combat, but rather of a life peopled by young men like **fallen angels,** and of a meteoric violence like that of **fallen angels,** beyond heaven or hell and partaking of both: doomed immortality and immortal doom. (young Bayard)

SAVIOR

Sartoris, 66:16
"... when de trouble bust loose, hit's 'Please, suh, Mr. Cullud Man; right dis way whar de bugle blowin', Mr. Cullud Man; you is de **savior** of de country.' " (Caspey to Simon)

Sartoris, 123:13
"Great **Savior**," he said, "where'd you have that demijohn hid? In your pants leg?" (proprietor of store to Rafe MacCallum)

Sartoris, 127:10
"Great **Savior**," he said, "them av'aytors was sure some hell-raisers, wasn't they?" (proprietor of store to young Bayard and Rafe Mac-Callum)

Sartoris, 144:31
"Great **Savior**, boy," he exclaimed, "ain't you gone home yet? Doc Peabody's been huntin' you ever since four o'clock, and Miss Jenny drove to town in the carriage, looking for you. You'll kill yourself." (proprietor of store to young Bayard)

SAVIORS

Soldiers' Pay, 12:26
"No," said Yaphank, "no! You have refused the hospitality of your train to the **saviors** of your country. We could have expected better treatment than this in Germany, even in Texas." (to train conductor)

Soldiers' Pay, 49:22

"Why, sure, General," Gilligan agreed readily. "She can't refuse one of the **saviors** of her country." (to Lowe re: Mrs. Powers)

SECT

Mosquitoes, 42:14

"And it is a human trait to foist the blunders of an age and the race upon some one or something too remote or heedless or weak to resist. But when you say religion, you have a particular **sect** in mind, haven't you?" (Semitic man to Fairchild)

SEED

Mosquitoes, 169:23

. . . this mist might have been the first prehistoric morning of time itself; it might have been the very substance in which the **seed** of the beginning of things fecundated . . . (F re: the swamp)

SEMITIC MAN

Mosquitoes, passim
Julius **"Semitic man"**, brother of Mrs. Eva Wiseman

SEPULCHRAL

Mosquitoes, 39:29

"And to be seduced by a girl in an orange smock and no stockings," the ghostly young man added in a **sepulchral** tone. (Mark Frost to Fairchild)

Mosquitoes, 44:4

"I am the best poet in New Orleans," the other interrupted with **sepulchral** belligerance. (Mark Frost to Talliaferro et al)

Mosquitoes, 262:33

"You guessed wrong again," Mark Frost said with **sepulchral** irony. (to Semitic man)

Mosquitoes, 330:5

He had completely forgotten about the niece: the **sepulchral** moth of his heart had completely forgotten that temporary flame. (Mark Frost and Patricia)

Mosquitoes, 334:1

. . . he . . . captured the practically whole cigarette which Miss Jameson had discarded. "Snipe," he murmured with **sepulchral** humorlessness and he fired it, averting his head lest he lose his eyelashes in doing so . . . (Mark Frost)

SEPULCHRALLY

Mosquitoes, 43:32

"I am invited, too," the blond young man put in **sepulchrally.** Mr. Talliaferro accepted him with apologic effusion. (Mark Frost)

Mosquitoes, 66:24

"Say he certainly ought to make Al Jackson a present of a bottle, oughn't he?" (Fairchild re: Major Ayers)
The thin poet groaned **sepulchrally.** (Mark Frost)

Mosquitoes, 231:13

"Sex and death," said Mark Frost **sepulchrally,** arcing the red eye of his cigarette, "a blank wall on which sex casts a shadow, and the shadow is life." (to Semitic man)

SERMON

Soldiers' Pay, 151:33

In the study where Donald sat, his father wrote steadily on tomorrow's **sermon.** The afternoon slept without. (rector and his son)

Soldiers' Pay, 169:11

His hands were clasped loosely upon the paper before him.
"Oh, you are writing a **sermon** and I have interrupted you. I didn't know," . . . (Mrs. Powers to rector)

Soldiers' Pay, 169:17

"Yes, yes. I will finish my **sermon** and join you." (rector to Mrs. Powers)

SERVICE

Mosquitoes, 37:1

"He is just the man to help you figure out some way to get God into the mercantile business. Teach him the meaning of **service,** hey, Talliaferro?" (Fairchild)

Mosquitoes, 41:1

"My people produced Jesus, your people Christianized him. And ever since you have been trying to get him out of your church. . . . Do you think that your new ideal of willynilly **Service** without request of recourse is better than your old ideal of humility?" (Semitic man to Fairchild et al)

SERVICES

Soldiers' Pay, 282:3

He conducted **services** in the dim oaken tunnel of the church while his flock hissed softly among themselves or slept between the responses . . . (F re: rector)

Soldiers' Pay, 318:28

. . . across a level moon-lit space, broken by a clump of saplings, came a pure quivering chord of music wordless and far away. "They are holding **services**. Negroes," the rector explained. (to Gilligan)

SHEPHERDS

Mosquitoes, 272:11

It is dawn, in the high cold hills, dawn is like a wind in the clean hills, and on the wind comes the thin piping of **shepherds,** and the smell of dawn and of almond trees on the wind. (F)

SHRINE

Sartoris, 179:16

. . . a gentle figure without legs or any inference of locomotion whatever, like a minor **shrine,** surrounded always by an aura of gentle melancholy . . . (Narcissa thinking about Horace)

SIN

Soldiers' Pay, 67:19

. . . Jones saw a thin face with a delicate pointed chin and wild, soft eyes. Jones' eyes were clear and yellow, obscene and old in **sin** as a goat's. (F comparing eyes of Jones and Donald)

Soldiers' Pay, 286:26

"Hush, Joe," Mrs. Mahon told him. Jones' eyes, clear and yellow, obscene and old in **sin** as a goat's, roved between them. (F)

Mosquitoes, 228:33

"I guess when you are young you have too much fun just being, to **sin** very much. But it's kind of nice, being young in this generation." (Fairchild to Semitic man)

Mosquitoes, 297:1

. . . and platters of spaghetti and roasted whole fowls, borne not by Joe, barearmed and skilful if taciturn, but by dinner-coated waiters with faces ironed and older than **sin** . . . (F re: restaurant of Pete and Joe)

Sartoris, 296:33

. . . Simon brought in . . . a cake baked cunningly with whisky and nuts and fruits and ravishing as odors of heaven and treacherous and fatal as **sin;** and . . . a bottle of port. (F)

SINFUL

Soldiers' Pay, 97:4

He was a Catholic, which was almost as **sinful** as being a republican; his fellow townsmen, while envying his social and financial position in the community, yet looked askance at him because he and his family made periodical trips to Atlanta to attend church. (F re: Mr. Saunders)

SINNER

Soldiers' Pay, 136:20
Jones rose and from a bookcase he got a copy of "Paradise Lost" (cheerful thing to face a **sinner** with, he thought), and returned to his chair. The chair was hard, but Jones was not. (F)

Sartoris, 24:7, 8
Sinner riz fum de moaner's bench,
Sinner jump to de pennance bench; . . . . (Elnore singing)

SINS

Mosquitoes, 228:32
"We were taught to believe that duty is infallible, or it wouldn't be duty, and if it were just unpleasant enough, you got a mark in heaven, sure . . . But maybe it ain't so different, taken one generation by another. Most of our **sins** are vicarious, anyhow." (Fairchild to Semitic man)

Mosquitoes, 229:4
"Not only are most of our **sins** vicarious, but most of our pleasures are too. Look at our books, our stage, the movies." (Semitic man to Fairchild)

Mosquitoes, 229:19
"It's the old problem of the aristocracy over and over: a natural envy of that minority which is at liberty to commit all the **sins** which the majority cannot stop earning a living long enough to commit." (Semitic man to Fairchild)

Sartoris, 199:29
. . . she had as many **sins** as her ordinary behavior could take care of, particularly as she had old Bayard's soul to get into heaven somehow also . . . (Miss Jenny)

SOLEMN

Soldiers' Pay, 66:17
This virgin shrieked at the spectacle of Jones, ludicrous in his shirt and his fat pink legs and the trousers jerked **solemn** and lethargic into the room. (F re: Emmy and Jones)

Mosquitoes, 82:30
. . . the Nausikaa at halfspeed forged slowly into a sluggish river mouth, broaching a timeless violet twilight between **solemn** bearded cypresses motionless as bronze. (F)

Mosquitoes, 218:6

Fairchild laughed his burly appreciative laugh. Then he met Major Ayers' glassy **solemn** stare, and ceased. (F)

Sartoris, 7:13

To the right of the entrance, beside folding doors rolled back upon a dim room emanating an atmosphere of **solemn** and seldom violated stateliness and known as the parlor, stood a tall mirror. . . . (F)

Sartoris, 19:11

But the door was closed now, and what light passed through the colored panes was richly **solemn**. To Bayard's left was . . . the room in which his grandson's wife and her child had died last October. (F)

Sartoris, 60:2, 4

And so it stayed closed nearly all the time, and slowly acquired an atmosphere of **solemn** and macabre fustiness. Occasionally young Bayard or John would open the door and peer into the **solemn** obscurity in which the shrouded furniture loomed . . . (F re: Sartoris parlor)

Sartoris, 180:10

The musty, **solemn** familiarity of calf-bound and never-violated volumes, on whose dusty bindings prints of Will Benbow's dead fingers might probably yet be found . . . (F re: Benbow library)

Sartoris, 315:11

From time to time during the meal a head would appear, staring above the rim of the box with blinking and **solemn** curiosity, then vanish with an abrupt scuffling thump . . . (F re: puppies at Mac-Callums)

Sartoris, 376:14

Well, it was the last one, at last, gathered in **solemn** conclave about the dying reverberation of their arrogant lusts, their dust moldering quietly beneath the pagan symbols of their vainglory and the carven gestures of it in enduring stone . . . (Miss Jenny at the cemetery)

SOLEMNITY

Sartoris, 375:4

. . . the inspiration and example of that one which dominated them all, which gave the whole place . . . an orotund **solemnity** having no more to do with mortality than the bindings of books have to do with their characters . . . (Miss Jenny in the cemetery)

SOLEMNLY

Soldiers' Pay, 17:21

"That's the horror of the demon rum, boys," said Yaphank **solemnly** and he took another drink. And Cadet Lowe took another drink. He tendered the bottle. (to traveling companions)

Soldiers' Pay, 235:19

Solemnly the clock on the courthouse, staring its four bland faces across the town, like a kind and sleepless god, dropped eleven measured golden bells of sound. (F)

Mosquitoes, 256:2

"Say, Josh, haven't you got a tool of some sort that'll get us off again?" The nephew regarded Fairchild **solemnly.**

Mosquitoes, 275:15

"That's it," said Fairchild **solemnly.** "Major Ayers guessed it the first time." (to Mrs. Maurier et al)

Sartoris, 56:32

Beyond a frame of sweet peas Isom in his khaki strode **solemnly** back and forth. Upon his right shoulder was a hoe and on his face an expression of rapt absorption, and as he reversed at the end of his beat he murmured to himself in measured singsong. (F)

Sartoris, 96:23

The doctor shut the cabinet carefully . . . with his thumbs hooked in his jacket pockets he became **solemnly** and unctuously technical, rolling the harsh words upon his tongue with epicurean deliberation. (F re: Dr. Alford after examining old Bayard)

Sartoris, 270:5

. . . the deputation came **solemnly** around the corner of the house from the rear. It consisted of six negroes in a catholic variety of Sunday raiment and it was headed by a huge, bull-necked negro in a . . . Prince Albert coat, with an orotund air and a wild, compelling eye. (F)

Sartoris, 297:1

But even Dr. Peabody allowed himself vanquished after a time, and then Simon brought in pies of three kinds, and a small, deadly plum pudding . . . and at last, with an air sibylline and **solemnly** profound, a bottle of port. (F)

Sartoris, 345:29

The children moved then and from the shadow behind them . . . they produced . . . a small mirror and a huge stick of peppermint candy to which trash adhered and which they immediately fell to licking **solemnly,** turn and turn about. (F re: three Negro children)

SOUL

Soldiers' Pay, 9:33

The man on the floor weeping said: "You wrong me as ever man wronged. Accuse me of hiding mortgage on house? Then take this **soul** and body; take all. Ravish me, big boy." (traveling companion to Lowe et al)

Soldiers' Pay, 16:26

"Well, bless my **soul**, if here ain't old Hank White in the flesh, that I was raised with! Why, Hank! We heard you was dead . . ." (Yaphank to Hank White)

Soldiers' Pay, 57:6

"But one of my cloth is prone to allow his own **soul** to atrophy in his zeal for the welfare of other souls . . ." (rector to Jones)

Soldiers' Pay, 290:17

Jones, sensing him, whirled in the dusk and Gilligan leaped upon him. "For the good of your **soul**," Gilligan told him joyously. "You might say that's what running with preachers does for you, mightn't you?" (to Jones)

Soldiers' Pay, 307:6

". . . when we get fed up all we need do is wish each other luck and go our ways." He stared at her, shocked. "Damn your Presbyterian **soul**, Joe." (Mrs. Mahon to Gilligan)

Mosquitoes, 18:16

"An artist? You flatter me, dear lady. I'm afraid my **soul** does not aspire so high. I am content to be merely a—" (Talliaferro to Mrs. Maurier)

Mosquitoes, 18:25, 27

"No, no; don't say you cannot: I am sure you are capable of it, what with your—your delicacy of **soul**, your—" . . . "Ah, to be a man, with no ties save those of the **soul**! To create, to create." (Mrs. Maurier to Talliaferro)

Mosquitoes, 25:22

"I like your red hair and beard. But you. You are black. I mean . . ." her voice fell and he suggested **Soul**? "I don't know what that is," she stated quietly. (Patricia to Gordon)

Mosquitoes, 47:7

. . . form by a madmans dream gat on the body of chaos le garcon vierge of the **soul** horned by utility o cuckold of derision. (Gordon)

Mosquitoes, 131:30

"And so do you, your poor emotional eunuch; so do you, despite that bastard of a surgeon and a stenographer which you call your **soul**, so do you remember with regret kissing in the dark and all the tender and sweet stupidity of young flesh." (Semitic man to Fairchild)

Mosquitoes, 183:18

"The art of Life, of a beautiful and complete existence of the **Soul**," Mrs. Maurier put in. "Don't you think that is Art's greatest function, Mr. Gordon?"

Mosquitoes, 184:1

"The **Soul's** hunger: that is the true purpose of Art. There are so many things to satisfy the grosser appetites." (Mrs. Maurier to Talliaferro et al)

Mosquitoes, 229:29

". . . all those traditional retreats that in the olden days enabled the church to produce a **soul** for every one it saved." (Semitic man to Fairchild)

Mosquitoes, 233:26

"The **soul** sheds every year, like snakes do, I believe. You can't recall the emotions you felt last year: you remember only that an emotion was associated with some physical fact of experience." (Fairchild to Semitic man et al)

Mosquitoes, 305:12, 12

Yes, Fairchild was right, he knew women, the feminine soul—? No, not **soul**: they have no souls. Nature, the feminine nature: that substance . . . impalpable as moonlight, challenging and retreating at the same time . . . (Talliaferro thinking)

Sartoris, 94:23, 23

The walls were an immaculate new gray . . . all impersonal and clean and inexpensive, but revealing at a glance the proprietor's **soul**; a **soul** hampered now by material strictures . . . (F re: Dr. Alford's office)

Sartoris, 143:23

These Suratt, who knew nearly every **soul** in the country, greeted with a grave gesture of his brown hand . . . (F)

Sartoris, 174:33

Aunt Sally was a good old **soul**, but she lived much in the past, shutting her mind with a bland finality to anything which had occurred since 1901. (F)

Sartoris, 199:30

Miss Jenny said . . . that she had as many sins as her ordinary behavior could take care of, particularly as she had old Bayard's **soul** to get into heaven somehow also . . . (F)

Sartoris, 200:1, 2

About young Bayard's **soul** Miss Jenny did not alarm herself at all: he had no **soul**. (F)

Sartoris, 223:6

His voice trailed away among ancient phantoms of the **soul's** and body's fortitudes, in those regions of glamorous and useless striving where such ghosts abide. (F re: old man Falls)

Sartoris, 279:12

Misunderstood even by that creature, the nigger who drives him . . . his inheritance is cooked away from him along with his **soul** in a glue factory. (F re: the mule)

Sartoris, 378:8

". . . he grabbed up that dawg that Abe shot last winter and laid its leg open and untangled them ligaments so quick that . . . even the dawg didn't know it 'til it was too late to holler. Only you forgot to dig a little further for his **soul,**" . . . (Dr. Peabody to Miss Jenny and his son, Loosh)

Sartoris, 378:12

"You don't know if he hasn't got one," young Loosh said, unruffled. "Dr. Straud has been experimenting with electricity; he says he believes the **soul**—" (to Dr. Peabody and Miss Jenny)

SOULLESS

Mosquitoes, 76:12

It was as beautiful as a racehorse and in a way terrifying, since with all its implacable **soulless** power there was no motion to be seen save a trivial nervous flickering of rockerarms . . . (F re: engine of boat, Nausikaa)

Mosquitoes, 83:5

The world was becoming dimensionless, the tall bearded cypresses drew nearer one to another across the wallowing river and the **soulless** implacability of pagan gods, gazing down upon this mahogany-and-brass intruder with inscrutable unalarm. (F re: the Nausikaa)

SOULS

Soldiers' Pay, 57:7

"But one of my cloth is prone to allow his own soul to atrophy in his zeal for the welfare of other **souls** . . ." (rector to Jones)

Soldiers' Pay, 58:28

"But who has ever found justice in youth, or any of those tiresome virtues with which we coddle and cradle our hardening arteries and **souls**?" (rector to Jones)

Soldiers' Pay, 196:20

This was the day of the Boy, male and female. (F)

"Look at them, Joe," Mrs. Powers said, "sitting there like lost **souls** waiting to get into hell." (at the dance)

Mosquitoes, 21:8

They rolled smoothly, passing between spaced lights and around narrow corners, while Mrs. Maurier talked steadily of hers and Mr. Talliaferro's and Gordon's **souls.** (F)

Mosquitoes, 25:25

. . . he suggested Soul? "I don't know what that is," she stated quietly.

"Neither do I. You might ask your aunt, though. She seems familiar with **souls**." (Patricia and Gordon)

Mosquitoes, 28:18

Damn their little **souls**, she whispered on a sucked breath. She yawned. (Patricia)

Mosquitoes, 184:20

"We do think they are lazy—just a little. Not mentally, but that their . . . not hearts—" "**Souls**?" her brother suggested. "I hate that word, but it's the nearest thing . . ." (Patricia and Josh to Julius et al)

Mosquitoes, 241:16

"You believe they have **souls**, then?" Fairchild asked.

"Certainly. If they are not born with them, its a poor creature indeed who can't get one from some man by the time she's eleven years old. (Semitic man)

Mosquitoes, 305:12

Yes, Fairchild was right, he knew women, the feminine soul—? No, not soul: they have no **souls**. (Talliaferro)

Mosquitoes, 305:19

As though the earth, the world, man and his very desires and impulses themselves, had been invented for the sole purpose of hushing their little hungry **souls** by filling their time through serving their biological ends . . . (Talliaferro thinking about women)

Sartoris, 9:18

. . . the history of the race had been raised from out the old miasmic swamps of spiritual sloth by two angels valiantly fallen and strayed, altering the course of human events and purging the **souls** of men. (F re: Aunt Jenny's story)

SPIRE (CHURCH)

Soldiers' Pay, 56:16

His shining dome was friendly against an ivy-covered wall above which the consummate grace of a **spire** and a gilded cross seemed to arc across motionless young clouds. (F re: rector)

Soldiers' Pay, 56:18

Januarius Jones, caught in the **spire**'s illusion of slow ruin, murmured: "Watch it fall, sir." The sun was full on his young round face. (to rector)

Soldiers' Pay, 56:27

"No, sir," replied Jones, "no aeroplane, sir. I referred in a fit of unpardonable detachment to your **spire**." (to rector)

Soldiers' Pay, 57:1

"It was ever my childish delight to stand beneath a **spire** while clouds are moving overhead. The illusion of slow falling is perfect. Have you ever experienced this, sir?" (Jones to rector)

Soldiers' Pay, 58:4

"Shall I let the stranger languish without my gates?" The grilled iron swung open and his earthy hand was heavy on Jones' shoulder. "Come, let us try the **spire**." (rector to Jones)

Soldiers' Pay, 58:7

A myriad bees vacillated between clover and apple bloom, apple bloom and clover, and from the Gothic mass of the church the **spire** rose, a prayer imperishable in bronze, immaculate in its illusion of slow ruin across motionless young clouds. (F)

Soldiers' Pay, 88:6

Young and miserable they clung to each other. The slumbrous afternoon lay about them in the empty lane. Even the sparrows seemed drowsy and from the **spire** of the church pigeons were remote and monotonous unemphatic as sleep. (F re: George Farr and Cecily)

Soldiers' Pay, 180:27

Pigeons in the **spire** were coolly remote from the heat, unemphatic as sleep . . . (F)

Soldiers' Pay, 181:11

It was because the sun was in her eyes that she couldn't see, sun going down beyond a lattice wall covered with wistaria. Pigeons crooned liquid gutturals from the **spire** slanting like smears of paint . . . (F re: Mrs. Burney)

Soldiers' Pay, 184:7

Sucking silver sound of pigeons slanting to and from the **spire** like smears of soft paint on a cloudless sky. (F)

Soldiers' Pay, 279:4

She looked quickly away, across the garden, beyond the **spire** where pigeons crooned the afternoon away, unemphatic as sleep, biting her lips. (Mrs. Mahon)

Soldiers' Pay, 282:6

He conducted services in the dim oaken tunnel of the church . . . while pigeons held their own crooning rituals of audible slumber in the **spire** that, arcing across motionless young clouds, seemed slow and imminent with ruin. (F re: rector)

Soldiers' Pay, 319:5

. . . they saw the shabby church with its canting travesty of a **spire**. Within it was a soft glow of kerosene . . . and from it welled the crooning submerged passion of the dark race. (rector and Gilligan)

SPIRES (CHURCH)

Soldiers' Pay, 176:25

He thought at times of Captain Green as he crossed France, seeing the intermittent silver smugness of rain . . . **spires** and trees; roads, villages; villages, towns, a city; villages, villages, then cars and troops . . . (Madden)

Mosquitoes, 14:4

Twilight ran in like a quiet violet dog and nursing his bottle he peered out across an undimensional feathered square . . . and three **spires** of the cathedral graduated by perspective, pure and slumbrous beneath the decadent languor of August and the evening. (F re: Talliaferro)

Mosquitoes, 48:33

Above banana and palm the cathedral **spires** soared without perspective on the hot sky. (F)

Sartoris, 372:24

When they reached town, from slender **spires** rising among trees, against the puffy clouds of summer, bells were ringing lazily. (F re: Miss Jenny and Isom)

SPIRIT

Soldiers' Pay, 29:23

"I was there in **spirit,** sweetheart. That's what counts." (Yaphank to Lowe)

Soldiers' Pay, 57:18

"My rebuke was tendered in the same **spirit** . There are certain conventions which we must observe in this world: one of them being an outward deference to that cloth which I unworthily, perhaps, wear." (rector to Jones)

Soldiers' Pay, 67:23

"There is always death in the faces of the young in **spirit,** the eternally young. Death for themselves or for others." (rector to Jones)

Soldiers' Pay, 187:22

But she had money—that panacea for all ills of the flesh and **spirit.** She believed in rights for women, as long as women would let her dictate what was right for them. (F re: Mrs. Worthington)

Mosquitoes, 26:2

"Do you see? The **spirit** of youth, of something fine and hard and clean in the world; something we all desire until our mouths are stopped with dust." (Talliaferro to Mrs. Maurier et al)

Mosquitoes, 26:21

"Oh, yes untrammeled." Here was a word Mrs. Maurier knew. "The untrammeled **spirit,** freedom like the eagle's." (Mrs. Maurier to Talliaferro et al)

109

Mosquitoes, 42:4

"But to go back to religion"—"the **spirit** protestant eternal," murmured the blond young man hoarsely—"do you mean any particular religion or just the general teaching of Christ?" (to Fairchild et al)

Mosquitoes, 125:18

. . . her unseeing eyes rested on his brown busy head while her **spirit** lay on its belly above Maggiore, watching . . . lonely arrogant eagles aloft in blue sunshot space surrounded and enclosed by mountains cloud brooded, taller than God. (Patricia and David)

Mosquitoes, 319:13

"Art reminds us of our youth . . . That's about all the virtue there is in art: it's a kind of Battle Creek, Michigan, for the **spirit**. And when it reminds us of youth, we remember grief and forget time." (Fairchild to Semitic man)

Sartoris, 1:4

As usual, old man Falls had brought John Sartoris into the room with him . . . fetching, like an odor, like the clean dusty smell of his faded overalls, the **spirit** of the dead man into that room where the dead man's son sat . . . (F re: old Bayard and his father)

Sartoris, 25:12

He descended and tethered the horses, and his **spirit** mollified by the rebuke administered and laved with the beatitude of having gained his own way, Simon paused and examined the motor car . . . (F)

Sartoris, 48:8

He was thinking of his dead brother; the **spirit** of their violent complementing days lay like dust everywhere in the room, oblitering that other presence, stopping his breathing and he went to the window . . . gulping air . . . (young Bayard re: John)

Sartoris, 175:16

He looked at her quickly, and the cloud faded from his face as suddenly as it had come, and his **spirit** slipped, like a swimmer into a tideless sea, into the serene constancy of her affection again. (Horace and Narcissa)

Sartoris, 280:2

Sometimes Bayard got out and went over and talked to him, leaving Narcissa in the car, lapped in the ripe odors of the failing year and all its rich . . . sadness, her gaze brooding on Bayard and the old negro . . . and her **spirit** went out in serene and steady waves, surrounding him unawares. (re: young Bayard)

Sartoris, 374:9

Yet withal there was something else, as though the merry wild **spirit** of him who had laughed away so much of his heritage of humorless and fustian vainglory managed . . . though his bones lay in an anonymous grave beyond seas, to soften the arrogant gesture with which they had bade him farewell . . . (F re: John Sartoris)

SPIRITUAL

Mosquitoes, 20:5
"He is quite shy, you know. Oh, quite, I assure you. Artistic temperament, you understand: so **spiritual** . . ." (Mrs. Maurier to Talliaferro et al re: Gordon)

Mosquitoes, 38:29
"As soon as a man begins to join clubs and lodges, his **spiritual** fiber begins to disintegrate. When you are young, you join things because they profess high ideals." (Fairchild to Semitic man)

Mosquitoes, 41:4
"The only ones who over gain by the **spiritual** machinations of mankind are the small minority who gain emotional or mental or physical exercise from the activity itself, never the passive majority for whom the crusade is set afoot." (Semitic man to Fairchild et al)

Mosquitoes, 251:8
"Interesting, anyway," the Semitic man said, "to reduce the **spiritual** progress of the race to terms of an emotional migration; esthetic Israelites crossing unwetted a pink sea of dullness and security." (to Mrs. Wiseman et al)

Sartoris, 9:16
. . . a gallant and finely tragical focal point to which the history of the race had been raised from out the old miasmic swamps of **spiritual** sloth by two angels valiantly fallen and strayed . . . (F)

SPIRITUALLY

Mosquitoes, 184:10
"Clinging **spiritually** to one little spot of the earth's surface, so much of his labor is performed for him. Details of dress and habit and speech . . . become quite as imposing as any single startling stroke of originality, as trivialities in quantity will." (Julius to Mrs. Wiseman et al)

SPIRITUALS

Soldiers' Pay, 313:1, 12
"Sweet chariot . . . comin' fer to ca'y me home . . ." . . .
". . . sweet chariot, comin' fer to ca'y me home . . . yes, Jesus, comin' fer to ca'y me hoooooome . . ." (Negroes singing)

Soldiers' Pay, 319:13, 14, 21

>Feed Thy Sheep, O Jesus. . . .
>Feed Thy Sheep, O Jesus. . . .
>Feed Thy Sheep, O Jesus. (Negroes singing)

Sartoris, 24:7

>Sinner riz fum de moaner's bench,
>Sinner jump to de pennance bench;
>When de preacher ax 'im whut de reason why,
>Say, "Preacher got de women jes' de same ez I."
>>Oh, Lawd, oh, Lawd!
>Dat's whut de matter wid de church today. (Elnora)

Sartoris, 42:11, 20

>"All folks talkin' 'bout heaven ain't gwine dar," . . .
>"All folks talkin' 'bout heaven ain't gwine dar." (Elnora)

STAR

Soldiers' Pay, 56:4

>Jones, Januarius Jones, born of whom he knew and cared not, becoming Jones alphabetically, January through a conjunction of calendar and biology, Januarius through the perverse conjunction of his own **star** and the compulsion of food and clothing . . . (F)

Mosquitoes, 153:29

>She coming into the dark sky of his life like a **star,** like a flame . . . O bitter and new . . . Somewhere within him was a dreadful laughter unheard . . . (Gordon)

Mosquitoes, 274:11

>(Your name is like a little golden bell hung in my heart, and when I think of you . . .) The Nausikaa sped on. It was twilight abruptly; soon, a **star.** (Patricia)

Sartoris, 18:8

>. . . Bayard Sartoris' brief career swept like a shooting **star** across the dark plain of their mutual remembering and suffering, lighting it with a transient glare like a soundless thunder-clap, leaving a sort of radiance when it died. (F re: Bayard Sartoris of Carolina)

Sartoris, 323:1

>In the sky no **star** showed, and the sky was the sagging corpse of itself. It lay on the earth like a deflated balloon . . . (F)

STARLIGHT

Mosquitoes, 335:16

>(In a doorway slightly ajar were women, their faces in the **starlight** flat and pallid and rife, odorous and exciting and unchaste . . .) (F)

Mosquitoes, 336:11
> (Fairchild stopped, laying his hand against the heat-drunken wall beside him, staring at his friend in the **starlight.** Gordon strode on ahead) ... (F)

Sartoris, 339:21
> Darkness overtook him soon, but he rode on beneath the leafless trees, along the pale road in the gathering **starlight.** (young Bayard on Christmas Eve)

Sartoris, 340:2
> On all sides the hills rolled blackly away in the **starlight** . . . they stood darkly towering and sinister overhead, lifting their leafless trees against the spangled sky. (F re: young Bayard on Christmas Eve)

Sartoris, 340:21
> The darkness spread away, lessening a little presently where occasional fields lay in the vague **starlight,** breaking the monotony of trees; and after a time . . . a cotton house squatted beside the road, its roof dusted over with a frosty sheen as of silver. (F re: young Bayard on Christmas Eve)

STARS

Soldiers' Pay, 187:29
> . . . they rolled smoothly beneath elms, seeing **stars** in a clear sky, smelling growing things, hearing a rhythmic thumping soon to become music. (F re: Mrs. Powers, Mahon and Gilligan in a car)

Soldiers' Pay, 196:3
> The music beat on among youthful leaves, into the darkness, beneath the gold and mute cacophony of **stars.** (F)

Soldiers' Pay, 196:6
> . . . **stars** were golden unicorns neighing unheard through blue meadows, spurning them with hooves sharp and scintillant as ice. (F)

Soldiers' Pay, 236:24
> It was as though vision were a bodiless Eye suspended in dark-blue space, an Eye without Thought, regarding without surprise an antic world where wanton **stars** galloped neighing like unicorns in blue meadows ... (George Farr)

Soldiers' Pay, 243:12
> The **stars** swam on like the mast-head of squadrons and squadrons on a dark river, going on and on. Darkness and silence and a world turning through darkness toward another day ... (F)

Soldiers' Pay, 314:20
> Branches motionlessly leafed were still against **stars,** and mopping his face and neck with his handkerchief he walked along a deserted street. (F re: Jones)

Mosquitoes, 47:30, 48:1

stars in my hair in my hair and beard i am crowned with stars christ by his own hand an autogethsemane carved darkly out of pure space . . . (Gordon)

Mosquitoes, 161:19

The skiff rose and fell against the stars, and mooned water bubbled about her. (F re: Patricia)

Mosquitoes, 162:2

The remote chill stars swung over them, and the decaying disc of the moon, over the empty world in which they clung by their hands, side by side. (F re: David and Patricia)

Mosquitoes, 163:6

He saw her flat boy's body against the stars rising, and she was in the boat, leaning down to him. (David and Patricia)

Mosquitoes, 292:17

The worn moon had risen and she spread her boneless hand upon the ceaseless water, and the cold remote stars swung overhead, cold and remote and incurious: what cared they for the haggard despair in his face, for the hushed despair in his heart? (F re: Talliaferro)

Mosquitoes, 305:32

And my nature is complex, he told himself, gazing at stars in the hot sky, in a path of sky above the open coffin of the street. (Talliaferro)

Mosquitoes, 335:8

(Gordon, Fairchild and the Semitic man walked in the dark city. Above them, the sky: a heavy, voluptuous night and huge, hot stars like wilting gardenias . . . .) (F)

Mosquitoes, 336:30

(. . . Above him, above the shallow serrated canyon of the street, huge hot stars burned at the heart of things.) (F re: Semitic man)

Mosquitoes, 338:7

(Fairchild walked erratically beside him. Above him, among the mad stars, Gordon's bearded head. The night was full and rich, smelling of streets and people, of secret beings and things.) (F)

Mosquitoes, 339:2

(. . . Gordon entered and before the door closed again they saw him in a narrow passageway lift a woman from the shadow and raise her against the mad stars, smothering her squeal against his tall kiss.) (F)

Mosquitoes, 346:16

But now as he walked dark streets beneath the hot heavy sky and the mad wilting gardenias of stars, feeling empty and a little tired and hearing his grumbling skeleton . . . (Talliaferro)

Sartoris, 10:15

. . . Stuart at thirty and Bayard Sartoris at twenty-three stood briefly like two flaming **stars** garlanded with Fame's burgeoning laurel and the myrtle and roses of Death . . . (F re: Aunt Jenny's story)

Sartoris, 179:5

. . . in the adjoining room Horace lay while that wild, fantastic futility of his voyaged in lonely regions of its own beyond the moon, about meadows nailed with firmamented **stars** to the ultimate roof of things . . . (F)

Sartoris, 205:17

It was like coming dazed out of sleep, out of the warm, sunny valleys where people lived into a region where cold peaks of savage despair stood bleakly above the lost valleys, among black and savage **stars.** (F re: young Bayard)

Sartoris, 254:7

Far above him now the peak among the black and savage **stars,** and about him the valleys of tranquillity and of peace. (F re: young Bayard)

Sartoris, 282:24

Overhead the **stars** swam vaguely in the hazy sky; the air was not yet chill, the earth still warm to the touch. (F re: a group hunting)

Sartoris, 282:29

They stood in a steady oasis of lantern light in a world of but one dimension, a vague cistern of darkness filled with meager light and topped with an edgeless canopy of ragged **stars.** (F re: a group hunting)

Sartoris, 314:18

He followed the others into the frosty darkness. Beneath his feet the ground was already stiffening; overhead the sky was brilliant with **stars.** (young Bayard)

SUNDAY

Mosquitoes, 41:17

"The only sense in which religion is general is when it benefits the greatest number in the same way. And the universal benefit of religion is that it gets the children out of the house on **Sunday** morning." (Semitic man to Fairchild et al)

Mosquitoes, 42:25

"How do young Protestant boys in small towns spend **Sunday** afternoons, with baseball and all such natural muscular vents denied them? They kill, they slay and steal and burn." (Semitic man to Fairchild et al)

115

Mosquitoes, 42:28, 29

"Have you ever noticed how many juvenile firearm accidents occur on **Sunday,** how many fires in barns and outhouses happen on Sunday afternoon?" (Semitic man to Fairchild et al)

Mosquitoes, 106:28

It was a single sheet of a **Sunday** magazine section: a depressing looking article in small print . . . (F)

Mosquitoes, 146:5

"Oh, yes. Well, we was at the Market. There was a big crowd there because it was **Sunday** night, see, and these other fellows was there. One of them was a snappy looking fellow, and I kind of looked at him." (Jenny to Patricia)

Sartoris, 270:1

It was a sunny **Sunday** afternoon in October. Narcissa and Bayard had driven off soon after dinner . . . (F)

Sartoris, 270:7

. . . the deputation came solemnly around the corner of the house from the rear. It consisted of six negroes in a catholic variety of **Sunday** raiment . . . (F)

Sartoris, 290:16

"Dat's de troof," Simon . . . in a collarless boiled shirt and his **Sunday** pants . . . and reeking a little of whisky in addition to his normal odors, agreed. (to young Bayard et al)

Sartoris, 330:11

He had a good tenor voice and was much in demand at **Sunday** singings. (F re: Lee MacCallum)

Sartoris, 371:22

She set the date before she went to bed and held to it stubbornly, refusing even to rise and attend the christening. That day fell on **Sunday.** (F re: Miss Jenny and young Bayard's child)

Sartoris, 376:12

. . . she watched a group of children playing quietly and a little stiffly in their bright **Sunday** finery, among the tranquil dead. (Miss Jenny at the cemetery)

SUNDAYS

Sartoris, 199:25

The duster and hat came down from the nail and the horses were harnessed to the carriage but once a week now—on **Sundays,** to drive in to town to church. (F)

116

SUNDAY SCHOOL

Soldiers' Pay, 231:1
". . . until I reached my eleventh year, the only time I ever knew passion was one day when I discovered beneath the imminent shadow of our annual picnic that my **Sunday school** card was missing." (Jones to Mrs. Saunders)

Soldiers' Pay, 231:17
"Since then I have been a firm believer in Christianity." (Jones) "How interesting," Mrs. Saunders commented . . . "I wish Robert liked **Sunday school** as much as that."

Mosquitoes, 34:16
Mr. Talliaferro ducked his head to a man with iron gray hair and an orotund humorless face like that of a thwarted **Sunday school** superintendent . . . (F)

TABERNACLE

Sartoris, 9:27
. . . once he hunted a pack of fox hounds through a rustic **tabernacle** in which a Methodist revival was being held; and thirty minutes later (having caught the fox) he returned alone and rode his horse into the ensuing indignation meeting. (F re: Aunt Jenny's story re: Bayard Sartoris of Carolina)

TEACHING OF CHRIST

Mosquitoes, 42:6
"But to go back to religion" _ "the spirit protestant eternal," murmured the blond young man hoarsely _ "do you mean any particular religion, or just the general **teaching of Christ?**" (to Fairchild et al)

TEMPLE

Soldiers' Pay, 283:2
They walked slowly in the garden along the avenue of roses which passed beneath the two oaks, beyond which, against a wall, poplars in a restless formal row were like columns of a **temple.** (Mrs. Mahon and Gilligan)

TEMPTATIONS

Soldiers' Pay, 59:7
"Had I the arranging of this world I should establish a certain point . . . which a man would be automatically relegated to a plane where his mind would no longer be troubled with the futile recollection of **temptations** he had resisted. . . . (rector to Jones)

Soldiers' Pay, 59:12

Jones, wondering what **temptations** he had ever resisted and then recalling the women he might have seduced and hadn't . . .

Mosquitoes: 115:29

". . . he found you a job near the college to pay your board, not enough to do anything else _ to keep you from fleshly **temptations,** you know _ and he had a monthly report on your progress sent to him." (Fairchild to Josh)

TESTAMENT (SEE ALSO OLD AND NEW)

Sartoris, 215:22

Soon a blaze, pale in the sunny air, and when the wood was burning strongly he laid the coat and the **Testament** and the trophy and the photograph on the flames . . . (young Bayard)

THANKSGIVING

Sartoris, 290:16

. . . Simon, propped in a slightly florid attitude against the sideboard, in a collarless boiled shirt and his Sunday pants (it is **Thanksgiving** Day) . . . (F)

Sartoris, 290:28

"I was talking to you, Loosh Peabody. You think just because you've eaten off of us **Thanksgiving** and Christmas for sixty years, that you can come into my own house and laugh at me, don't you?" (Miss Jenny)

Sartoris, 291:28

This was the pint flask of whisky which he included in old man Falls' **Thanksgiving** and Christmas basket and which the old fellow divided out by spoonfuls as far as it would go among his ancient and homeless cronies . . . (old Bayard)

THOU (GOD)

Mosquitoes, 345:5

"O **Thou** above the thunder and above the excursions and alarms, regard Your masterpiece!" (Fairchild to Talliaferro)

TIME (ETERNITY)

Soldiers' Pay, 5:4

Soldier
"The hushed plaint of wind in stricken trees
   Shivers the grass in path and lane
And Grief and **Time** are tideless golden seas _
   Hush, hush! He's home again." (F)

Soldiers' Pay, 144:14

A negro driving a wagon passed between them, interminable as **Time**: he thought the wagon would never pass, so he darted around it to overtake her. (F re: Cecily and George Farr)

Soldiers' Pay, 151:27

Negroes humped with sleep . . . a pagan catafalque under the afternoon. Rigid, as though carved in Egypt ten thousand years ago. Slow dust rising veiled their passing, like **Time** . . . (F)

Soldiers' Pay, 152:23

Donald Mahon knowing **Time** as only something which was taking from him a world he did not particularly mind losing, stared out a window into green motionless leaves: a motionless blur. (F)

Soldiers' Pay, 170:4

Mahon sat motionless, hopeless as **Time,** as across the grass came an old negro woman, followed by a strapping young negro in a private's uniform. (F)

Soldiers' Pay, 225:14, 16

The golden sand of hours bowled by day ran through the narrow neck of **time** into the corresponding globe of night, to be inverted and so flow back again. Jones felt the slow black sand of **time** marking his life away. (F re: Jones)

Soldiers' Pay, 293:3

. . . a day that had long passed, that had already been spent by those who lived and wept and died, and so remembering it, this day was his alone: the one trophy he had reft from **Time** and Space. (Donald Mahon)

Soldiers' Pay, 312:29

The cabins were dark but from them came soft meaningless laughter and slow unemphatic voices cheerful yet somehow filled with all the old despairs of **time** and breath. (F)

Mosquitoes, 10:33

Spring and the cruellest months were gone, the cruel months, the wantons that break the fat hybernatant dullness and comfort of **Time**; August was on the wing, and September—a month of languorous days regretful as woodsmoke. (F)

Mosquitoes, 164:6

The first morning of **Time** might well be beyond this mist, and trumpets preliminary to a golden flourish . . . (F)

Mosquitoes, 174:10

. . . this puny descration of a silence of air and earth and water ancient when hoary old **Time** himself was a pink and dreadful miracle in his mother's arms. (F)

Sartoris, 1:9

Freed as he was of **time** and flesh, he was a far more palpable presence than either of the two old men who sat shouting periodically into one another's deafness ... (F re: old John Sartoris, old man Falls, old Bayard)

Sartoris, 74:5

... then he was dead . . . who had not waited for **Time** and its furniture to teach him that the end of wisdom is to dream high enough not to lose the dream in the seeking of it. (re: young John Sartoris)

Sartoris, 92:12, 12

Old Bayard sat for a long time, regarding the stark . . . apotheosis of his name. Sartorises had derided **Time,** but **Time** was not vindictive being longer than Sartorises. (F)

Sartoris, 347:6

Bayard sat in his hard chair and dozed the morning away—not sleep, but **time** was lost in a timeless region where he lingered unawake and into which he realized after a long while that something was trying to penetrate. . . . (F)

TIMELESS (ETERNAL)

Mosquitoes, 82:30

... the Nausikaa at halfspeed forged slowly into a sluggish river mouth, broaching a **timeless** violet twilight between solemn bearded cypresses motionless as bronze. (F)

Mosquitoes, 177:22

The swamp did not seem to end, ever. On either side of the road it brooded, fetid and **timeless,** somber and hushed and dreadful. (F)

Mosquitoes, 212:2

Her voice was muffled by her arms, and after it, there was no sound in this fecund, **timeless** twilight of trees. (F re: Patricia)

Mosquitoes, 225:11

... feeling all familiar solid things fall away from under her and seeing familiar faces and objects arc swooping away from her as she plunged from glaring sunlight through a **timeless** interval into Fear like a green lambence straying to receive her ... (Jenny)

Mosquitoes, 243:13

"For by getting himself and his own bewilderment and inhibitions out of the way by describing ... American life as American life is, it will become eternal and **timeless** ..." (Semitic man to Mark Frost et al)

Mosquitoes, 339:24

... that instant of **timeless** beatitude, which some never know, which some, I suppose, gain at will, which others gain through an outside agency like alcohol ... (Gordon to Fairchild)

Sartoris, 347:7

... time was lost in a **timeless** region where he lingered unawake and into which he realized after a long while that something was trying to penetrate ... (old Bayard)

TREES OF HAVEN

Sartoris, 352:15

But as he sat musing, gazing out of the window where, beyond a tarred roof that drank heat like a sponge and radiated it, against a brick wall a clump of ragged **trees of heaven** lifted shabby, diffident bloom ... (Horace)

TRINITY MOTIF

Mosquitoes, 21:27

So against his better judgement he struck matches for them, leading the way up the dark tortuous stairs while their **three shadows** aped them, rising and falling monstrously upon the ancient wall. (Mr. Talliaferro, Mrs. Maurier and Patricia)

Mosquitoes, 335:1

Three gray, softfooted **priests** had passed on, but in an interval hushed by windowless old walls there lingers yet a thin celibate despair. (**F**)

Mosquitoes, 335:6

(**Gordon, Fairchild and the Semitic man** walked in the dark city. . . .) (**F**)

Mosquitoes, 335:13

The **three priests** pass on: the walls have hushed their gray and unshod feet. (**F**)

Mosquitoes, 335:30

I love **three things.** (**F**)

Mosquitoes, 336:6

I love **three things.** (**F**)

Mosquitoes, 336:32, 337:1

Three more **priests,** barefoot, in robes the color of silence, appear from nowhere. They are speeding after the first **three,** when they spy the beggar beneath the stone gate. (**F**)

Mosquitoes, 338:13, 16

The **three priests** gaze at one another. ... I love **three things:** gold, marble and purple. (**F**)

Mosquitoes, 339:8

(They went on. The Semitic man nursed the bottle against his breast.) I love **three things**.... (F)

Mosquitoes, 340:11

(The Semitic man nursed the bottle against his breast. "I love **three things**: gold, marble and purple—") (F)

Sartoris, 345:12

The **three children** squatted against the wall ... without movement and without sound. "Christmas come yet, chillen?" he asked them. But they only stared at him with the watchful gravity of animals ... (young Bayard to Negro children)

TRUMPET

Soldiers' Pay, 243:26

There was a rumor of light eastward, somewhere beyond her house and the room where she lay in the soft familiar intimacy of sleep, like a faintly blown **trumpet** ... (F re: Cecily)

Soldiers' Pay, 252:5

Spring, like a soft breeze, was in the rector's fringe of hair as with upflung head he tramped the porch like an old warhorse who hears again a **trumpet** after he had long thought all wars were done. (F)

Soldiers' Pay, 298:4

Outside the window, afternoon became abruptly rain, without warning, with no flapping of pennons nor sound of **trumpet** to herald it. (F)

Soldiers' Pay, 299:9

Outside the window the afternoon became abruptly rain, without warning, with no flapping of pennons nor sound of **trumpet** to herald it. (F)

TRUMPETS

Soldiers' Pay, 225:12

The **trumpets** in his blood, the symphony of living, died away. (F re: Jones)

Mosquitoes, 164:7

The first morning of Time might well be beyond this mist, the **trumpets** preliminary to a golden flourish; and held in suspension in it might be heard yet the voices of the Far Gods on the first morning saying, It is well: let there be light. (F)

Mosquitoes, 166:11

The mist without thinning was filling with light: an imminence of dawn like a glory, a splendor of **trumpets** unheard. (F)

Sartoris, 344:5

His movements were stiff and awkward and he descended the ladder slowly and gingerly into the red sun that fell like a blare of **trumpets** into the hallway. (young Bayard in the barn Christmas morning)

UNCTION

Soldiers' Pay, 311:25

"You'll get used to it, though. Take another." He drank it like water, with **unction**. (companion and Gilligan)

Mosquitoes, 109:19

Pete turned in the narrow corridor, counting discrete identical doors. He smelled coffee and he added to himself: A hard trip, and, with **unction:** I'll tell the world it is. (F)

UNCTUOUS

Mosquitoes, 52:11

"Oh, well, we Nordics are at a disadvantage," Fairchild replied. His tone was **unctuous**, the other detected something falsely frank in it. (to Semitic man et al)

Mosquitoes, 66:31

"Why, didn't you ever hear of Al Jackson?" asked Fairchild in **unctuous** surprise. "He's a funny man, a direct descendent of Old Hickory that licked you folks in 1812, he claims." (to Major Ayers et al)

UNCTUOUSLY

Mosquitoes, 98:3

Fairchild heaved himself off the bunk and got Mr. Talliaferro a tumbler. Mr. Talliaferro drank it slowly, **unctuously;** and pressed, accepted another. (F)

Sartoris, 96:24

The doctor shut the cabinet carefully . . . and with his thumbs hooked in his jacket pockets he became solemnly and **unctuously** technical, rolling the harsh words upon his tongue with epicurean deliberation. (Dr. Alford)

UNHOLY

Sartoris, 258:13

Be care full I am a desparate man Nothing any more to me now If you **unholy** love a man I will kill him. (letter to Narcissa from an admirer)

UNICORNS

Soldiers' Pay, 196:6
... stars were golden **unicorns** neighing unheard through blue meadows, spurning them with hooves sharp and scintillant as ice. (F)

Soldiers' Pay, 236:25
It was as though vision were a bodiless Eye ... regarding without surprise an antic world where wanton stars galloped neighing like **unicorns** in blue meadows. (George Farr)

UNWINGED

Sartoris, 175:26
The meaning of peace. Old unchanging days; **unwinged** perhaps, but undisastrous, too. You don't see it, feel it, save with perspective. (F)

VERITIES

Sartoris, 168:17
"Still, they've just gone through with an experience that pretty well shook the **verities** and the humanities, and whether they know it or not, they've got another one ahead of 'em that'll pretty well finish the business." (Horace to Narcissa re: the Sartoris family)

VIRGIN

Soldiers' Pay, 225:25
... Jones ... a religio-sentimental orgy in gray tweed, shaping an insincere, fleeting articulation of a damp clay to an old imperishable desire, building himself a papier mache **Virgin** . . . (F)

VIRTUE

Mosquitoes, 230:33
The Semitic man grunted. Mark Frost said: **"Virtue** through abjectness and falsification: immolation of insincerity."

VIRTUES

Soldiers' Pay, 58:27
"But who has ever found justice in youth, or any of those tiresome **virtues** with which we coddle and cradle our hardening arteries and souls?" (rector to Jones)

Soldiers' Pay, 60:32
His arm was heavy and solid as an oak branch across Jones' shoulder. "Tell me, what do you consider the most admirable of **virtues**?" (rector to Jones)

WINGED

Soldiers' Pay, 291:25
... the woman's dark dress shaped her against the dull white of her canvas chair. Her face was pallid, **winged** either side by her hair. (Mrs. Mahon)

Mosquitoes, 187:11
... ay ay strangle your heart o israfel **winged** with loneliness feathered bitter with pride. (F)

Sartoris, 151:1
Bayard's head was as cool and clear as a clapperless bell. Within it that face emerged clearly at last: those two eyes round with grave astonishment, **winged** serenely by two dark wings of hair. (young Bayard)

WINGS

Soldiers' Pay, 22:23
Outside the station in the twilight the city broke sharply its skyline against the winter evening and lights were shimmering birds on motionless golden **wings,** bell notes in arrested flight ... (F)

Soldiers' Pay, 31:6
Beneath his scar the officer slept in all the travesty of his **wings** and leather and brass ... (F re: Donald Mahon)

Soldiers' Pay, 45:24, 24
To have got **wings** on my breast, to have **wings;** and to have got his scar, too, I would take death to-morrow. (Julian Lowe re: Donald Mahon)

Soldiers' Pay, 45:26
Upon a chair Mahon's tunic evinced above the left breast pocket **wings** breaking from an initialed circle beneath a crown, tipping downward in an arrested embroidery sweep; a symbolized desire. (F)

Soldiers' Pay, 45:30
To be him, to have gotten **wings,** but to have got his scar too! (Julian Lowe re: Donald Mahon)

Soldiers' Pay, 111:16
(S'what I say: if the Lord had intended folks to fly around in the air He'd 'a' give 'em **wings.**) (townspeople)

Mosquitoes, 76:18
... the very bulkheads trembled with it, as though a moment were approaching when it would burst the steel as a cocoon is burst, and soar upward and outward on dreadful and splendid **wings** of energy and flame. (F re: engine of boat)

125

Mosquitoes, 165:5
Here, at the water level, she could see nothing save a grayness and flaccid disturbed tongues of water lapping into it, leaving small fleeting gaps between mist and water before the mist filled them again silently as settling **wings.** (F re: Patricia)

Mosquitoes, 186:26
Noon was oppressive as a hand, as the ceaseless blow of a brass hand: a brass blow neither struck nor withheld; brass rushing **wings** that would not pass. (F)

Mosquitoes, 187:1
But the unbearable hiatus of noon passed at last and the soundless brazen **wings** rushed westward. (F)

Mosquitoes, 188:9
The sunlight was beginning to slant at last, slanting westward like a rushing of unheard golden **wings** across the sky ... (F)

Mosquitoes, 215:22
... soon they had passed from the bronze nave of the river onto the lake beneath the rushing soundless **wings** of sunset and a dying glory of day under the cooling brass bowl of the sky. (F re: David and Patricia)

Mosquitoes, 268:7
And he went on down the passage with a singing lightness in his heart, a bright silver joy like **wings.** (F re: Gordon)

Mosquitoes, 268:25
"But you came back," ... (Patricia)
"And so did you," he reminded her from amid his soundless silver **wings.** (Gordon)

Mosquitoes, 269:15
... the silver **wings** in his heart were touched with pink and gold while he stood and looked downward upon the coarse crown of her head ... (F re: Gordon and Patricia)

Sartoris, 133:3
The beast burst like bronze unfolding **wings;** the onlookers tumbled away from the gate and hurled themselves to safety as the gate splintered to matchwood beneath its soaring volcanic thunder. (F re: the stallion)

Sartoris, 149:13
Hub bent forward and reached his hand under the dash, and the car swept on with a steady, leashed muttering like waking thunderous **wings** ... (F)

Sartoris, 156:24
When they had gone, she came to the window and parted the cur-

tains and stood for a while in the dark fallen **wings** of her hair, looking directly into his hidden eyes. (Narcissa and caller)

Sartoris, 172:10
He emerged at last, in a white shirt and serge trousers, but still borne aloft on his flaming verbal **wings** ... (F re: Horace)

Sartoris, 176:23
Her hair was smoother than any reposing **wings,** sweeping with burnished unrebellion to a single knot low in her neck. (F re: Narcissa)

Sartoris, 374:16
'I bare him on eagles' **wings**
and brought him unto Me' (epitaph of Lieutenant John Sartoris)

WISDOM

Mosquitoes, 233:31
"Experience: why should we be expected to learn **wisdom** from experience? Muscles only remember, and it takes repetition and repetition to teach a muscle anything. . . ." (Fairchild to Semitic man)

Sartoris, 178:23
"But then, acquired **wisdom** is a dry thing; it has a way of crumbling to dust where a sheer and blind coursing of stupid sap is impervious." (Horace to Narcissa)

WISE MAN

Mosquitoes, passim
Mrs. Eva **Wiseman,** guest on the Nausikaa

WORD

Mosquitoes, 130:25, 27
"It's the **word** that overturns thrones and political parties and instigates vice crusades, not things: the Thing is merely the symbol for the **Word.**" (Semitic man to Fairchild)

WORD OF GOD

Mosquitoes, 242:25
"They have sat among their objects, transcribing their Greek and Latin and holding correspondences across the Atlantic, but they still found time to put out of their New England ports with the **Word of God** in one hand and a belaying pin in the other ..." (Mrs. Wiseman to Semitic man)

ZEAL

Soldiers' Pay, 57:6
"But one of my cloth is prone to allow his own soul to atrophy in his **zeal** for the welfare of other souls ..." (rector to Jones)

APPENDIX A

EXPLETIVES OF RELIGIOUS ORIGIN

AND

CASUAL OR INCIDENTAL USES

BLESS

Soldiers' Pay, 11:24, 16:25, 42:6, 135:23, 298:31, 306:17

CHRIST

Soldiers' Pay, 8:18, 33, 14:18, 15:8, 26:9, 27:6, 47:26, 51:14, 174:2, 13, 200:30

Mosquitoes, 194:9, 345:16

CURSE

Soldiers' Pay, 70:27

Sartoris, 264:22

CURSED

Soldiers' Pay, 70:23, 73:32, 178:5, 291:11, 313:11

Mosquitoes, 22:10, 215:13, 302:25

Sartoris, 127:24, 143:3, 210:8

CURSING

Soldiers' Pay, 145:26, 178:14, 217:18, 304:7, 308:22

Mosquitoes, 282:29

Sartoris, 5:2, 209:32

DAMN

Soldiers' Pay, 13:22, 14:27, 23:21, 28:29, 36:26, 40:4, 27, 43:13, 63:8, 75:13, 78:18, 21, 82:7, 84:29, 86:7, 91:25, 99:19, 100:15, 103:25, 110:32, 112:26, 113:6,23, 130:22, 134:30, 141:23, 147:27, 150:4,6, 159:23, 168:4, 174:7,14, 205:31, 214:13, 223:9, 226:22, 227:5, 229:24, 230:3, 240:11, 246:11,18, 250:18,23, 251:14, 252:23, 253:13,14,16,32, 255:26, 283:16, 291:28, 294:25, 301:6, 302:20, 306:14, 307:6, 311:26, 313:29, 316:23

Mosquitoes, 48:7,8, 92:8, 95:5, 165:19, 181:1, 193:20, 194:2,21, 195:27, 196:25, 202:7, 212:23, 230:9, 256:32, 257:19, 271:10, 276:1, 301:16, 307:31, 316:10, 329:11, 330:2, 341:4, 344:7, 345:7

Sartoris, 5:33, 20:22, 30:17, 34:4, 44:14,27,29, 45:22,25,27,32, 75:16, 98:32, 104:2, 126:9, 127:21, 128:16,19, 131:3, 142:6,18, 146:13, 152:21, 160:30, 168:29, 172:2, 191:20,27,31,32, 192:1,3,10, 210:1, 8,13, 214:3, 220:14, 223:28, 227:32, 233:1, 237:22,25,29, 243:16, 20, 244:1,3, 251:1, 262:4, 271:28, 292:23, 305:10, 310:33, 311:2,18, 324:10, 328:15, 335:22, 336:23, 355:6, 360:29, 362:28

DAMNED

Soldiers' Pay, 32:11, 70:26, 97:24,25,32, 132:19, 246:16, 248:20

Mosquitoes, 85:5, 114:4,6,15, 285:28, 322:21,23

Sartoris, 85:5, 87:22,25, 99:28,32,33, 140:14, 146:15, 227:9,23, 234:3,5, 236:24, 242:19, 271:27, 272:1, 306:25, 308:18, 336:19,20

DEVIL

Soldiers' Pay, 163:25, 182:28, 223:2, 306:33

Mosquitoes, 18:18, 130:28

Sartoris, 167:20, 205:3, 227:7, 230:16, 233:30, 308:31

DEVILS

Soldiers' Pay, 198:32

Mosquitoes, 131:15, 199:14

GOD

Soldiers' Pay, 12:4,30,32, 14,9,32, 15:6, 25:17, 29:30, 45:15,16, 46:16, 47:13, 48:1,5, 84:28, 85:14, 117:31, 143:27, 150:11, 169:2,8, 174:13, 182:4, 183:14, 212:13,13,32,33, 223:20, 242:14, 268:22, 24, 297:25, 310:33

Mosquitoes, 11:3,6, 40:7, 58:22,24, 108:22, 141:6, 186:7, 193:5, 246:17, 250:22, 257:6, 275:2, 306:23, 329:11, 341:5, 342:13, 343:1, 348:23

Sartoris, 13:4, 52:1, 84:18,25, 104:8, 128:16, 164:33, 210:1,13, 245:29, 246:1, 261:32, 292:16, 305:5, 360:6, 369:26

GODDAM

Soldiers' Pay, 9:7,20, 12:18, 31:24, 39:7, 47:18, 145:25, 174:11,20, 192:14, 209:9, 212:18, 226:22, 227:15, 252:23

Mosquitoes, 80:26, 257:9

Sartoris, 18:25,28, 43:30, 46:13

GOD'S SAKE

Soldiers' Pay, 11:31, 13:32, 48:19, 88:30, 168:15

Mosquitoes, 46:27, 61:12, 308:18

Sartoris, 17:21, 129:12, 230:3

HEAVEN

Soldiers' Pay, 7:21, 188:15, 242:15, 305:3

Mosquitoes, 210:23

Sartoris, 84:18, 185:34

HEAVENS

Mosquitoes, 20:14

HELL

Soldiers' Pay, 7:22, 8:19, 9:28,29, 10:22,29, 14:31, 20:9, 22:8, 23:21, 24:3,29,32, 25:11, 29:26, 33:21, 40:25, 43:6, 47:16,18,20, 51:24, 53:12,14,16, 54:12, 55:14, 76:27, 83:14, 85:5,18, 89:25, 91:15, 100:17, 103:23, 145:18, 146:7, 167:4, 168:18, 173:19,21, 174:18, 175:7, 176:7, 178:9, 194:30, 195:29, 196:17, 210:6, 223:13, 236:11, 240:6,12, 241:17, 242:7, 243:4, 251:14, 253:15, 17, 265:23, 268:23, 307:15, 310:20, 311:19, 313:19, 316:4,12

Mosquitoes, 12:9, 66:15, 115:13, 131:33, 149:16,30, 193:17,20, 209:16, 217:22, 257:20, 279:11, 281:7, 283:7, 299:3,6,14, 308:11, 345:10

Sartoris, 8:8, 44:3, 48:30, 114:34, 125:32, 126:13, 127:26, 145:1, 160:27, 160:35, 200:16, 317:8

JESUS

Mosquitoes, 202:11

JESUS CHRIST

Soldiers' Pay, 10:16

Mosquitoes, 192:32, 194:8

LAWD

Soldiers' Pay, 170:22, 170:30

Sartoris, 8:11, 50:18, 82:16,29, 87:13

LORD

Soldiers' Pay, 43:31

Mosquitoes, 51:10, 133:9, 136:23, 137:8, 139:26, 142:28, 148:15, 150:28, 156:30, 177:6, 264:8, 323:24, 331:19, 342:22

Sartoris, 84:12, 89:4, 151:19, 165:9, 262:20, 276:11, 325:11, 379:22

SOUL

Soldiers' Pay, 91:25, 135:23, 253:33, 313:29

Mosquitoes, 165:19

Sartoris, 128:16

APPENDIX B

CHARTS RELATED TO THE SELECTED

RELIGIOUS ALLUSIONS FOUND IN:

SOLDIERS' PAY

MOSQUITOES

SARTORIS

ALLUSIONS	SOLDIERS' PAY	MOSQUITOES	SARTORIS	Totals	Percents
Metaphysics, cosmos, divinity, God, heaven, hell, time	96	92	90	278	15.8
Christ, religious doctrine, faith, ethical and moral aspects	57	88	119	264	15
Bible and Biblical personages	9	12	11	32	1.8
Church history, organization, sects, offices, officers	49	33	27	109	6.2
Religious beliefs and practices related to Negroes	16		38	54	3
Rituals and ceremonies	38	12	60	110	6.3
Church architecture, religious artifacts	47	18	11	76	4.3
Symbolic, metaphoric motifs and parallels	62	154	75	291	16.6
Expletives of religious origin	233	106	147	486	27.7
Casual, incidental uses of religious materials	10	3	36	49	2.8
Totals	617	518	614	1749	
Percents	35.2%	29.6%	35.1%		

ALLUSIONS IN SOLDIERS' PAY, MOSQUITOES, SARTORIS

Metaphysics, cosmos, divinity, God, heaven, hell, time	Soldiers' Pay	
	Mosquitoes	
	Sartoris	
Christ, religious doctrine, faith, ethical and moral aspects	Soldiers' Pay	
	Mosquitoes	
	Sartoris	
Bible, Biblical	Soldiers' Pay	
	Mosquitoes	
	Sartoris	
Church history, organization, sects, offices, officers	Soldiers' Pay	
	Mosquitoes	
	Sartoris	
Religious beliefs and practices related to Negroes	Soldiers' Pay	
	Mosquitoes	
	Sartoris	
Rituals, ceremonies	Soldiers' Pay	
	Mosquitoes	
	Sartoris	
Church architecture, religious artifacts	Soldiers' Pay	
	Mosquitoes	
	Sartoris	
Symbolic, metaphoric motifs and parallels	Soldiers' Pay	
	Mosquitoes	
	Sartoris	
Expletives of religious origin	Soldiers' Pay	
	Mosquitoes	
	Sartoris	
Casual, incidental uses of religious materials	Soldiers' Pay	
	Mosquitoes	
	Sartoris	

Scale — 1 inch = 40

TOTAL ALLUSIONS IN SOLDIERS' PAY, MOSQUITOES, SARTORIS

Metaphysics, cosmos, divinity, God, heaven, hell, time	Soldiers' Pay / Mosquitoes / Sartoris
Christ, religious doctrine, faith, ethical and moral aspects	Soldiers' Pay / Mosquitoes / Sartoris
Bible and Biblical personages	Soldiers' Pay / Mosquitoes / Sartoris
Church history, organization, sects, offices, officers	Soldiers' Pay / Mosquitoes / Sartoris
Religious beliefs and practices related to Negroes	Soldiers' Pay / Mosquitoes / Sartoris
Rituals, ceremonies	Soldiers' Pay / Mosquitoes / Sartoris
Church architecture, religious artifacts	Soldiers' Pay / Mosquitoes / Sartoris
Symbolic, metaphoric motifs and parallels	Soldiers' Pay / Mosquitoes / Sartoris
Expletives of religious origin	Soldiers' Pay / Mosquitoes / Sartoris
Casual, incidental uses of religious materials	Soldiers' Pay / Mosquitoes / Sartoris

Scale — 1 Inch = 80

ALLUSIONS	Soldiers' Pay	Mosquitoes	Sartoris	Totals
Bible	9	7	7	23
Christ	13	8	6	27
Christmas		9	39	48
Church	19	15	21	55
Fate, Doom	15		18	33
God	21	15	10	46
Heaven	9	7	13	29
Hell	15	11	13	39
Providence		9	7	16
Soul	13	23	14	50
Old Testament	33	23	23	79
New Testament	18	11	36	65

PROTESTANT ALLUSIONS

	Soldiers' Pay	Mosquitoes	Sartoris	Totals
Baptist	4		3	7
Deacon			2	2
Episcopal	2			2
Minister	4		2	6
Preacher	2		3	5
Preachers	1	2		3
Presbyterian	1			1
Protestant		5		5
Puritans		1		1

CATHOLIC ALLUSIONS

	Soldiers' Pay	Mosquitoes	Sartoris	Totals
Catholic	2	2		4
Cathedral	1	6		7
Priest	3	5		8
Priests		8		8

APPENDIX C

MIRRORS OF CHARTRES STREET

In the sketches which he contributed to the *Times Picayune* in the spring of 1925,[1] when he was writing *Soldiers' Pay*, we have many indications that Faulkner was experimenting in them with the ways in which Christian allusions and terms might be used to add emotive and dramatic values to what otherwise would have been merely local color sketches. In the first of these sketches, "Mirrors of Chartres Street," we have a thumbnail portrait of a familiar Chartres Street character, in this case, an old beggar whose ugly and decrepit outer appearance contrasts with certain spiritual attributes. For example, the cripple "swung himself across my path with ape-like agility," but his eyes are "as wild and soft as a faun's." Later he is seen "swinging himself into a movie theatre" where he wasted the money on one of "those million-dollar pictures of dukes and adultry and champagne." But Faulkner sees him not as a debauched materialist really, but as "an untrammelled spirit," related first of all to the life-affirming spirit of "young Jesus of Nazareth" and second to the Christian dreams that inspired the legends of "King Arthur and the Crusades." However, although the sketch might end on this note, it does not. For even here we see Faulkner's characteristic pursuit of a theme, which he encircles, defines, redefines, and sifts through myriad perspectives of time and a variety of observers. Later we see the old cripple again, this time against the background of a reference to the Vorticists—it is moonlight and the planes of light and shadow are clear to the "despair" as Faulkner puts it, of the Vorticist schools. Against this moonlit backdrop, the cripple revolves "like a water beetle about a rock" as a policeman attempts to arrest him. There follows a tirade in which the cripple "stood miraculously on his single leg and his crutch spun about his head like a propeller blade." He speaks foolishly and bitterly of his American rights, of his interest in Sam Gompers. He calls the cop a damn Republican. But he finally submits to the arrest. And the sketch ends, not on the note of Jesus of Nazareth at all, but on a reference to pagan Rome, in which the policeman is seen as reminiscent of "Caesar mounting his chariot among cast roses . . . while beggars crept out to see and centurions clashed their shields in the light of golden pennons flapping across the dawn." In other words, the pagan values prevail where materialism prevails.

The second of these sketches is an account of the narrator's encounter with a race track tout. They go to the track together, where the tout becomes involved in a bitter argument with a rival tout. When the narrator wins, both touts appeal warmly for his continued friendship, although each is really more interested in the rivalry which binds them together in hostility. Again, although nothing really happens in the sketch, we see Faulkner investing it with multiple meanings, most of them derived from religious allusions. First of all, much of the discussion centers around the St. Charles

---

[1] Reprinted as *Mirrors of Chartres Street, Faulkner Studies*, (Minneapolis, Minnesota, 1953). Introduction by William Van O'Conner.

hotel. The first tout is Jewish. He pretends to live at the St. Charles. Meetings are always arranged at the St. Charles, where we may even assume the narrator does live, although the point is left obscure. The narrator is amused and intrigued by the Jewish tout's constant use of the St. Charles as a symbol of respectability and at one point says "I was interested in seeing if he really could get in the St. Charles, even in a democracy . . ."

When they take a cab, the driver refuses to believe that the Jew can live at the St. Charles and when the tout threatens to have him arrested, he says, "You wouldn't no more dare call a cop than you'd dare go to the St. Charles."

The driver then asks the narrator whether he lives at the St. Charles. Nothing happens. "We seemed to have been caught in some horrible vaccum of inactivity . . ." Finally he has to resort to asking the tout whether it is incredibly true that he does live at the St. Charles. After a time we learn that the truth is that he lives not at the hotel itself but at the Alhambra Baths right next door. In this somewhat crude sketch the tout is portrayed as a Semite reminiscent on a lower level of the Semitic man in *Mosquitoes*. He is a degraded Hebraist with an obsessional devotion to race track winnings. He is indifferent to his own appearance, to his comfort, or to his peace of mind. Yet, he constantly refers to himself as a gentleman—"I have been a chentleman all my life." He also uses a phrase which appears frequently throughout the series—a corrupted spelling of Jesus, spelled "Cheest," a phrase which becomes the title of the fourth sketch in the series.

Cheest is a slang expression with the tout—his most common one. But when he is pressed by the young jockey rival, he can cry in "utter anguish" as Faulkner puts it, "as God is my witness . . ." The rival tout is his junior by many years. He is referred to as "the boy." At the end of the sketch the Semite is seen glowering at his son-rival, whose name we learn is McNamara, all but oblivious to the fact that he and the narrator are to meet the following day "at the St. Charles, at twelve sharp." Again the name of the hotel is used to provide an ironic religious backdrop to the pathetic materialistic rituals.

In these first two published sketches, then, Faulkner uses Hebraic-Christian terminology and allusion primarily as an ironic overtone, letting them lend religious flavor to a world momentarily preoccupied with materialism and beset by a kind of money-fetishism.

In the other sketches in the series other purposes emerge, but the line of allusion remains constant. The third, for example, is called "Home." The central character is a former French soldier, Jean-Baptiste—the degraded counterpart of John the Baptist. Jean remembers bitterly the war which convinced him "that all fighting troops had been thrust into purgatory for some unnamed sin . . ." He remembers too the irony of the French priest blessing the shells. "Let these shells scatter the enemies of France . . . before the wind, O Lord." He remembers that much of the hell and purgatory of

140

the war stemmed from a man like himself, a Corsican with the warm Southern blood in his veins. Then Jean-Baptiste is brought out of his revery by a Creole musician who spends his days singing provencal songs on Chartres Street, accompanying himself with a violin bow played on a carpenter's saw. He remembers now not war, but "the wooded hills and valleys, willow and tall chestnuts in the meadows" and he realizes suddenly that he had sought his destiny across seas when he might have found it in his village home as a boy, a fact which "three years in the mud of Artois and Champagne could not make him see." Here the religious terms are not used ironically, but serve rather to provide an aesthetic based on the moral of tranquillity.

The fourth sketch might well be termed an experiment in the language of sacrilege. Its title "Cheest" sets off a first person narrative in which the speaker is a Northern jockey named Jack Potter. To him as to the tout in the second sketch, this vulgarization of Jesus is an automatic verbal response. He uses it again and again in telling a tale of racing and jockeys in which the influence of some of Sherwood Anderson's tales is apparent.

After this slight and unfinished piece, we move into quite a different one called "Out of Nazareth." Here the tone is devotional and the method more clearly suggestive of the later Faulkner devices. Faulkner and his artist friend, Spratling, the painter, who incidentally did a volume of sketches called "Sherwood Anderson and Other Creoles" to which Faulkner contributed a preface, are watching the drifters sitting around Jackson Park. They enter the park under "immaculate shapes of lamps." They notice the old men who "had learned that living is not only not passionate or joyous, but is not even especially sorrowful." Then they see the young protagonist; "his young face brooded upon the spire of the Cathedral." Spratling calls him a David. They find that he is, in fact, a migratory worker. After talking to him they learn that he is a devoted reader of Housman's *Shropshire Lad*, and that he has written an account of his recent travels which he wants to give to Faulkner when he learns that he is "a writing man." Though he is American, "he could have come from anywhere, and probably had. He was eternal, of the earth itself."

They try to help him, and Spratling suggests that he go home. But he is indifferent. And now Faulkner switches to the boy's own narrative, which he prints without charge. "There is bad punctuation here, and misspelling ...But to correct it would ruin it."

It is a story of wandering on the open road, Whitmanesque in both style and theme with obvious resemblance to "Song of Myself."

"With a pack on my back (consisting of necessary articles rolled into two blankets) I trudge along. The smell of farmhouse fires drifts down the wind to me. Pure air fills my lungs and gives an exileration unlike any other that I know. The morning sun casts long shadows across the fields. The dew of early morning glitters and the tall grass overhanding the side of the road is heavy with it. . . .

141

"I have slept well on dried corn stalks between long rows of corn. I need not travel. I have no destination. I am at peace with the world.

"I have my thoughts as a companion.

"As the sun creeps higher the glare of summer is reflected from long rows of yellow corn . . . I sweat. Great drops roll down my face and settle in my open collar. The heat is good. It loosens the legs and warms the ground for the night' sleep.

"Miles slide behind me . . . Why should I ask for rides when all around me is content? Those who wish to help me may do so, others may go on their way. I have no destination. Why should I hurry?

"All afternoon I loll on the back seat of a speeding car (who's owner had invited me to ride). There is a dog in the back seat with me and we converse together as best we may . . . I stop for a minute to watch the changing form of some hill and he gently nudges me with his nose. My hand returns to his head and we resume our comradie . . ."

Later the boy describes a camp of migrants, not hoboes, but migrants seeking work. Among them are a German actor, a young Swede from Dakota, "a thin-face gangling Arkansan" who is moving now from West to East, from Vancouver and California "and we'll get there prit' soon if Pop don't haf' to stop and get a job carpentering to buy us gas and food."

When Faulkner takes up the narrative again, he editorializes more explicitly than he does elsewhere in the series. What he admires most in the boy is "his beautiful faith that life, the world, the race, is somewhere good and sound and beautiful." It is all something that "is good to see." Thus it is that this sketch, published in the *Picayune* for April 12, 1925, might be regarded as the central piece in the group. It is, indeed, the most explicitly affirmative statement of what might best be called a primitive Christian ethic. And it is part of a group written especially for the Easter season. The next, "Kingdom of God," appeared on April 26, and the following one, "The Rosary," was published on May 4.

A later sketch called "The Cobbler," which appeared on May 10, may be regarded as the last of an Easter series. It returns again to the mood "Out of Nazareth." This time the narrator is an Italian from Tuscany who remembers with affection his life as a shepherd and of his love for the young girl to whom he was betrothed. She is "treading out the grapes in the autumn . . . as though dear Christ Himself had bathed her feet in His own dear blood." But the marriage does not come to pass, for a wealthy gentleman comes to the village and she was lost to him. He has only now a withered yellow rose that she gave him. But the rose renews his love and his faith yearly. "The saints are very good," he concludes. "Was I sad? I do not know. I have known joy and sorrow, but now I do not remember. I am very old: I have forgotten much."

"The Kingdom of God" is interesting mainly because it contains an episode unnoticed by critics which was later to become the concluding section of *The Sound and the Fury*. It is an account of a pair of bootleggers, one of whom has had to bring along an idiot brother who like Benjy in the

142

later novel breaks into "deafening" howls because a beloved narcissus flower is broken in the haste of the men to escape from the police. At the end of *The Sound and the Fury*, Benjy cannot be given a new flower after his is broken because as Luster says, "Y'all took all of um Friday to decorate the church." Luster then fixes a splint for the broken flower stem. In "The Kingdom of God" the brother gets the policeman to allow him to find a "small sliver of wood. String was volunteered by a spectator, who fetched it from a nearby shop; and under the interested eyes of two policemen and the gathering crowd the flower stalk was splintered. Again the poor damaged thing held its head erect and the loud sorrow went at once from the idiot's soul. His eyes were like two scraps of April sky after a rain and his drooling face was moonlike in ecstasy."[2]

In "The Rosary" the tone is again ironic for it refers not to the Catholic symbol but rather to the popular hymn, which in this sketch is particularly despised by a Mr. Harris, a Protestant, and admired by his Catholic neighbor, a Senor Juan Ventura. The hatred of Harris toward Venturia has all of the zeal and determination of the religious wars, but when Mr. Harris becomes ill and dies Juan belatedly decides to play "The Rosary" outside his room. Harris is now dead, but the Catholic plays on, his rendition so off-key that no one recognizes the song, and only he realizes that it is "The Rosary" he is playing.

I have said before that these sketches were written while Faulkner was working on *Soldiers' Pay*. In that book, too, the church plays a predominant part. The rector, the church grounds, the use of the scarred young veteran as a faceless symbol of all mankind are elements in a larger thematic structure which cannot be analyzed here. However, in all of the work Faulkner produced during the first half of 1925, devices and techniques which reach much more elaborate development in his later work are clearly in evidence.

In sum, then, the *Chartres Street* series seem to indicate first of all that Faulkner was from the beginning concerned with developing his themes and his style in terms of the Hebraic-Christian tradition, specifically through rhetorical and symbolic uses of religious terms and allusions. In "Out of Nazareth" we have an explicit statement of an affirmative faith in man, seen in the context of primitive Christianity which comes close to Faulkner's philosophical position. Throughout this series and in *Soldiers' Pay*, the good is seen as the natural, the generous, the courageous, and the beautiful, and the evil as the obsessed, the materialistic, the hypocritical, and above all the shallowly proud.

These early sketches are often crude and unfinished, and they range from a tone of irony and even farce to one of devotional sincerity. But they are important. There are phrases in the *Chartres Street* sketches which

---

2 The parallel passage in *The Sound and the Fury* read: "Ben quit simpering. He sat in the middle of the seat, holding the repaired flower upright in his fist, his eyes serene and enviable . . ." But in *The Sound and the Fury*, the flower symbol is broken again, after the disastrous mistake Luster made in turning the carriage to the left of the Confederate monument, a mistake corrected by Jason in time to prevent utter chaos, but with fatal damage to the flower, now broken beyond repair.

143

anticipate the Nobel Prize speech. There are episodes which anticipate the themes of later work. And, above all, there is in these sketches much of the philosophy, of the rhetorical patterns, and of the conceptions of character which find their ultimate development in what is unquestionably Faulkner's major work, *A Fable.*